The Souls of Poor Folk

Edited by
Charles Lattimore Howard

Preface by Dennis P. Culhane
Afterword by James Spady
Illustrated by David White

UNIVERSITY PRESS OF AMERICA, ® INC.
Lanham • Boulder • New York • Toronto • Plymouth, UK

Copyright © 2008 by
University Press of America,® Inc.
4501 Forbes Boulevard
Suite 200
Lanham, Maryland 20706
UPA Acquisitions Department (301) 459-3366

Estover Road
Plymouth PL6 7PY
United Kingdom

Library of Congress Control Number: 2007934503
ISBN-13: 978-0-7618-3856-2 (paperback : alk. paper)
ISBN-10: 0-7618-3856-2 (paperback : alk. paper)

The Souls of Poor Folk is collection of essays that in the tradition of Dr. DuBois' classic *Souls of Black Folk*, move between the scholarly, the narrative and the testimonial. This text is meant to be a small contribution to the critical dialogue around ways to alleviate poverty in our world. The contributors are diverse not only in their experience and origin, but in their perspectives and beliefs about the appropriate means to engage poverty and its many causes.

As there are indeed a myriad of causes and paths to poverty, it would make sense to engage them on diverse fronts. This is the reasoning behind the Greater Love Project: Vol. 1: The Souls of Poor Folk.

The Greater Love Project Vol. 1: The Souls of Poor Folk is a multimedia initiative of Greater Love Movement and Peace of Music that is engaging listeners, viewers, and readers with thoughtful and challenging perspectives on the various aspects of poverty and homelessness in America. These messages are reaching their audience via the following vehicles: an original music compilation (CD), an original film documentary (DVD), a published collection of original essays and an interactive website. Through this coordinated effort, artists, scholars, social service providers, and other concerned citizens will reach a large portion of our society and encourage them to live their lives with care, concern, and remembrance of those who are far too often forgotten. www.thesoulsofpoorfolk.org

Contents

7 Silent Pulpits: A Historical Examination of Black Christian
Engagement with Capitalism
Charles Lattimore Howard

Preface

In the last three years, we have been tragically reminded of our collective frailty on this planet and in this country. The tsunami on December 26, 2004, and Hurricane Katrina in 2005 brought devastation to hundreds of thousands of people. Beyond the sheer magnitude of the human toll, these disasters also taught us many things about ourselves. When disasters of this nature strike, they may seem at first to be indiscriminate, taking everyone in their wake. But upon closer examination, we can see that natural disasters such as these expose a far more discomforting portrait of grief, of people whose lives of poverty and marginality have been made visible to us only in their death and dislocation. While certainly many of the victims of these disasters were not poor, the concentration of risk among the poor is what is so disturbing, and yet so illuminating.

With some exceptions, the same can be said of other disasters—social and biological. Tuberculosis and human immunodeficiency virus, for example; however broad or localized they may be in the population at first, they end up concentrated among the poorest people among us, among people whose lives at the margins might otherwise be forgotten, were it not for the devastation their exposure brings, and its risk to " the rest of us." Drug abuse. Homicide. Homelessness. Accidental injury. Hazardous waste exposure. War casualties. All of these phenomena have a "class" gradient, and given the interrelatedness of race and class in the US, an apparent race dynamic as well.

In the aftermath of Hurricane Katrina, many of us wanted to point the finger of blame at the incompetence of FEMA, and there was plenty to point at. The agency's bureaucratic lethargy, the basic lack of preparedness for this specific threat, and the lack of logistical foresight were glaringly obvious. But, even FEMA's incompetence is as much a symptom as a problem. The

Army Corps of Engineer's failure to adequately protect New Orleans from a storm surge was also as much a symptom as it was a problem. The failure of the Indian Ocean nations (and the world) to have a basic early warning system in place for detecting earthquakes on the ocean floor, that would predict tsunamis and activate evacuation plans for coastal settlements, is another symptom as much as a problem. The deliberate relegation of poor people in the US to homeless shelters and the failure of our social safety net to otherwise protect people from destitution is as much a symptom as a problem.

After all, the fact that storms hit, diseases emerge, or that poverty afflicts, is not surprising. To the contrary, these events are to be expected. What is so vexing is that it is our human responses, and even the very ways we have deliberately organized our societies—things we presumably can control—that have damned so many people, unnecessarily, to exposure and loss in the face of these predictable events. Catastrophes rarely result from an external threat alone (though certainly some do). They also result from a tragic failure to exercise the political and social will necessary to prepare, to plan, and to protect, in the face of quite predictable exposures.

The underlying processes that place poor and marginalized people at inordinate risk of exposure to disasters and that isolate them in the face of their suffering, are the very problems that create poverty and marginalization in our society in the first place. These underlying processes may not be singularly visible events like hurricanes and tsunamis, but they are just as real and catastrophic. Indeed, they are perhaps even more deadly, because they operate more or less invisibly, in the day to day functioning of our housing and labor markets, and in the machinations of government policy. Unfortunately, the often stark inequalities that result, even when disturbingly visible, are not very disturbing to many people at all. Insolated geographically, socially, and ideologically, many of us are content to ignore the harsh realities meted out by our daily exchange of goods, services, work and income (and their lack), and the larger systems of maldistribution which underlie them.

Worse still, our public spheres, primarily government and other social policy arenas, where the risks associated with class and inequality and the broader interests of "the public" should be taken foremost into consideration, are often so overwhelmed with a narrow self-interest as to contribute to, rather than ameliorate the collective risk posed by the hidden systems of class. Thus grinds on the machinations of daily life, placing people at risk of poverty, in unsafe housing, in flood plains, in disaster- or hazard-prone environments, in dangerous work, in areas lacking adequate infrastructure to support prevention activities, in areas lacking warning systems, and in social systems lacking in the basic logistics of protection or the amelioration of loss.

From this perspective, the ordinariness and everydayness of our social systems of reproduction are as disturbing as the problems that ultimately result from more fantastic events. Equally disquieting are the seductive justifications offered by the ideological and meritocratic codes embedded in everyday life, that reinforce our ideas that the poor deserve their lot, and that "the rest of us" deserve our superior and safer positions.

But not the readers of this book. This book is intended as a thoughtful and provocative disturbance. The contributors have crafted essays which do not aim to please. Chaz Howard has compiled a group of essays that collectively question the social, political and economic processes that produce marginality, which recast and re-privilege the so-called marginal, and which offer new inspirations and directions. As the contributors collectively extol, we cannot justifiably sit idly, letting the day-by-day world go by, letting endemic social disasters such as homelessness persist, or letting natural disasters strike those who could otherwise be protected. These past and present catastrophes have taught us that critical reflection and study are necessary in understanding how and why our human systems could fail, and fail so many, so miserably. This book is part of that process. And may critical action closely follow.

Dennis P. Culhane, Ph.D. -2007

Acknowledgements

SOLI DEO GLORIA

This project, like so many in life I am finding, turned out to be very different than we had originally envisioned it. It was meant to be much more factual and even systematic in its engagement with poverty looking at distinct factors that contribute to it (education, lack of affordable housing, unlivable wages, etc.) However, it has emerged as a much more narrative piece with reality translated from numbers to names. Like the original *Souls*, this work moves from narrative to academic to testimonial — with recurring themes and challenges. I don't think Dr. DuBois would be disappointed with this and neither are we. Still, we recognize that this is very much only the beginning — not even. This is rather just another step along the way towards bringing some relief to the unnecessary poverty in the world, if not towards alleviating it altogether.

It is with sincere gratitude that I thank all of the contributors to this volume for sharing their vision, their experiences, and their passion. I am grateful for Dr. Culhane's invaluable support and encouragement of Greater Love over the years as well as for the work that he does on behalf of poor peoples everywhere. Love to James Spady and the entire Umum crew (H. Samy Alim, Samir, Dave White, Leandre and all fam in the Cipha). Mr. Spady stands as one of the leading journalists and writers of the last few decades and as a powerful mentor in my life. I am thankful for my dear friend Capt. Andrew Exum not only for his strong essay, but for the service he has provided by risking his life on behalf of others. Salute! Rev. Debbie Little-Wyman is a living saint and has been one of the most influential individuals on me vocationally. Brooke Beck's kindness to my family (my daughter's godmother!) has given me a small glimpse into the generosity of love and spirit that she has shared with people literally around the world. Prof. Beth Lyon's work in the courtroom and in the classroom have meant much to me and to many others. And Rev. Erik Williams' message of radical grace and love is one that we all need to hear. I am delighted to have witnessed my friend and brother share this message to all God's children. Special thank you to Rob Murat for sharing your musical gifts with the world and with this project. "Souls" is a powerful piece and I'm so pleased you let us wrap the project in it. And to Dave White and Yaminah McKessy for the way you speak powerfully through your art and for your very generous support and kindness through this process.

The fingerprints and influence of so many others are all over this project. Rev. William Gipson, Sr. Mary Macrina, Rev. Dr. Kirk Jones, Dr. Ben Valentin, Dr. Greg Mobely, Rev. Dr. Katie Day, Rev. Dr. Stephen Ray, Rev. Dr. John Hoffmeyer, Dr. Michael Dyson, and Dr. Cornel West (all of the above remain my advisors and mentors). Valerie, Karlene, Anita, Nathan, Fran, Rodney, Larry, Rabbi Mike, Sean, Leah, Jim, President Gutmann and President Rodin for your kindness during my Penn Days. Thanks to Rose of Sharon and Good Samaritan. To Alpha, especially Rich and Curtis. To Andover Newton Theological School and to Lutheran Theological Seminary of Philadelphia. To Steve, Masi, Daron, Coach Forman, Coach Holly, Coach Duncan, Finney, Montgomery, McGill and all of Gilman for so much foundation. To LaToya, Rachel, and all Greater Love Folks. My man Nathan, Ali and Peace of Music. Derrick, San No, Dean Krych, and so many others.

To Ovie and CPH Sr. To Bishop Turner, to my mother and father who walk with me daily. To my Sisters Ami, Trina, and Cara and my Brothers Charles, Dana, John, and Mark. To John and Christine, Aunt Betty and Uncle Lonnie, Shanea, Aunt MiMi, Joe, Yvonne, Gwen and all family from Baltimore to Plainfield to California. To my girls Charissa Faith and Annalise Hope. But most importantly to my wife Lia, whose unfailing love has meant so much to me over the last several years. You are my miracle and your love has strengthened my faith.

This volume is written for the glory of God and dedicated to

Martin Luther King Jr.—Paul Robeson—
Adam Clayton Powell, Jr.—W.E.B. DuBois

Mbaraka Wa Mungu

The Forethought

Herein lie many things which if read with patience may show the strange meaning of being poor here in the dawning of the Twenty-first Century. This meaning is not without interest to you, Gentle Reader; for the problem of the Twenty-first Century is the problem of the poverty line.

High above, the wealth of the earth is traded and accumulated and held in deep pockets and wide purses and large accounts. So many stories below, millions of stories interlock forming a chain which to some is freedom and love and to others is slavery and cruelty. These stories are the wisdom of souls and wounds of bodies which bruise the souls within.

Between me and the other world there is an ever unasked question: unasked by some through feelings of delicacy; by others through the difficulty of rightly forming it. All, nevertheless flutter around it.

They avoid me the way pedestrians change paths so as not to step in trash on the sidewalk. And occasionally some eye me curiously or compassionately, and then, instead of saying directly, "How does it feel to be a problem—to be a blemish on the face of our city—to be unemployed, or an addict, or crazy, or lazy, or whatever got you out here? . . .Yes instead of saying any of that they just look with their eyes . . . or they don't. Or maybe they give me a few coins or their leftovers from a meal just picked at. At these I smile, or am interested, or reduce the boiling to a simmer as the occasion may require. To the real question, how does it feel to be a problem? I answer seldom a word.

And yet being homeless—being poor, is a strange experience especially in one of the wealthiest nations/kingdoms the world has ever seen. It is in the early years of my twenties that the revelation first bursts upon me all in a day, as it were. I remember well when the Ruah swept across me.

Faces I cannot remember, only ankles and cars driving by as I chased after sleep that would not come. My arm on the sidewalk served as my pillow. I replayed conversations over and over and each time tears fell. In the end it was not alcohol or my unlivable salary that pinned me to the ground, but it was a broken heart and what I thought was an orphaned soul.

And there was no solace. No not one of them stopped to ask why I wept or why I was lying on the sidewalk. They passed by. Glanced maybe. Some even crossed the street—something I have experienced as a man of color. Now I feel it as a poor man despised with a slightly different fear.

No visions of weddings in my eyes, but now I see with a new clarity just how the veil hangs. This veil over our faces—hindering us from greeting each other. And it is not beautiful. Not adorned with jewels and flowing. No, this one is gray. You can't even see our faces, but I pray that you will see our souls.

Chapter One

Long Ways From Home: Motions, Memories and Katrina's Storm Surge

James G. Spady

Ain't no pain
Ain't no strain
Gonna get in the way

Ain't no rain
No Hurricane
Gonna put us away

—*"Souls" Rob Murat*

The Economist reporter's voice over in London is heard loud and clear: "Since Katrina, the world's view of America has changed. The disaster has exposed some shocking truths about the place; the bitterness of its sharp racial divide, the abandonment of the dispossessed, the weakness of critical infrastructure. But the most astounding and most shaming revelation has been in the government's failure to bring succor to its people at their time of greatest need."[1] Even before Katrina touched its shores, many African Americans in the Gulf Region were already at the center of a mighty hurricane as they sought opportunity and relief from extremities of racism, poverty and elitism. Levees in their lives had already been broken as had dreams, promises and memories. Mahalia joins Clara in singing, "How I Got Ovah." And now it is time for Yolanda Adams and Beyonce to sing Katrina's sacred/secular song as homeless survivors move on with their lives. Souls look back and wonder hot they got ovah.

No street lights. No lights of any kind. All we can see is darkness. All we can hear is the flowing of a rushing tide as water fills the streets of the city. Nawleeeeens. Darkness covers the earth and it is without light or form. Destinies locked inside of racial memories. Astonishing. Shaming. Abandoned.

Dispossesed. Packed along the levee since the flood of 1927. Where will they be pushed in the New New Orleans 2007? Backwater Blues. Only poets like Juvenile, Lil Scrappy, Lil Wayne, Turk, B.G. and Sonia Sanchez can capture their humanity. Lonely and forsaken in the wilderness of North America. Marie Laveau is not pleased. Randolph Desdunes, James Borders and Marcus Christian saw it coming. Where is Mannie Fresh when we need that Bounce Hop track to keep us moving? David Banner strikes the very nerve of it all. Mannie flees to ATL to link up with Young Jeezy who is at the very eye of the storm. The changing same.

No Name in the Streets and no lights in New Orleans. Faceless, lightless and forgotten. And yet they want to tell their story. Name tags and arm bands are needed. Strangers in a strange land. Who are these heroines and heroes? Who are these sun blessed people who survived Hurricane Katrina and the levee explosion in 2005 and what can we learn from their unforgettable stories? New Orleans, Gulfport and Biloxi form the figurative backdrop for a sobering, surrealistic narrative of epic magnitude.

WITNESS #1, JEREMY COLLIER

Wayblackmemories: " My Moms had left for Atlanta. I was working. I had got off that morning. I worked from 8 o'clock that night until 8 o'clock in the morning. So I came home and it was nothing happening. It was just a little rain." That is how Jeremy Collier of Jefferson Parish, Louisiana describes the relative calm before the storm. What began as 'just a little rain' became one of the most tragic natural disasters in the history of the United States. It was further worsened by governmental neglect at the local, state and federal levels. In reflecting on how this disaster impacted his life, Jeremy states, ' So I went to sleep. In the morning when I woke up, I saw trees and water. Everything in excess. So I'm like, 'What's going on?' So I cut on the radio and it kept telling me it's real. It's going to happen. But by the time I woke up, the lights were gone. My cell phone wasn't working. It was working but it wasn't getting no signal because of the hurricane and all of that.' That is the testimony of Witness #1, Jeremy Collier.[2]

Asked to describe everyday life in New Orleans before the hurricane, John Fernandez of the now devastated 9th Ward, declares: " Life in New Orleans' 9th Ward is just like in any other area. You've got the good and you've got the bad."[3] This Saturday afternoon, Fernandez and several other Katrina evacuees met Philadelphia musicians Jill Scott, Musiq, Hansoul, Freeway, Bilal, Young Gunz, Floetry, Ms. Jade, Jaguar Wright, Tye Tribbett & Greater Anointing and Peedi Crakk. Fernandez later comments, " Jill Scott is real. I didn't expect for her to walk up and talk to us like she did on this level like that."

FROM ST. BERNARD PROJECTS TO NORTH PHILLY

Edward Allen enters the Katrina Discourse Cipha; remembering, reconciling and revivifying more and more memories. Allen speaks with the emotional force and speed of a West African harmattan: "I'm from St. Bernard Projects. I'm in the 7th Ward. I left on the flight from New Orleans on Tuesday. I left my house that Sunday before anything happened and I went to the hotel. My girlfriend's daddy was the supervisor at the hotel. It was nice at the beginning but it turned out bad. People killing people in there! Yeah! Man, crazy ain't the word. I watched a man get shot up in the parking lot. Watching that. 'Pow Wow.' Gone! He was hit but he got up and ran. Next day, you could see him floating. This was Tuesday or Wednesday. My girlfriend and I escaped and we came here. Her daddy went to Illinois."[4]

"HOW AM I GOING TO EVACUATE WHEN I AIN'T GOT NOWHERE TO EVACUATE TO?"

Many questions have been raised about the City of New Orleans' failure to evacuate the nearly half million people trapped in a deadly hurricane. Why didn't more residents evacuate? When that question was put to Edward Allen, he responds in an animated manner: "Let me go back to the evacuation. I heard everybody was going to evacuate. How am I going to evacuate when I ain't got nowhere to evacuate to? I wasn't going to no Superdome! All them people got killed up there. I ain't about to go get supered up! If I'm going to die, I might as well be at home. I ain't going to try to starve to death. I had food and water in the hotel. All them people down there. Couldn't even dig a hole and bury the people! You can't help but remember that, man. And it took three days for help to come. I couldn't get in touch with my Mama and them. They were still at the house. I asked my Grandma if she wanted to come and live in the hotel. Mom and them were going to the Superdome but they changed their minds. See, the Creator looked out for them. My Grandma stayed in the Project because she thought she would be okay. The water got so deep you couldn't walk in it and you couldn't go swimming in there either. My Grandma, she old. I didn't want her to be in that." When asked where his grandmother is now, Allen responds with another question, "Where Grandma at now? She in the hospital in Houston somewhere. They had to rescue her out of the projects."[5]

Allen ends with what seems to be a constant among nearly all of those who managed to get out of New Orleans and other Gulf Region States hit by Katrina—a concern for the well being of their families. Blacks who survived this horrific experience have made the concern for family and the reuniting of black families a priority and a subject of discussion by mass media journalists. Even those who escaped could not bear leaving the region without making sure that their families were safe. Edward Allen makes this crystal clear when he says, "I was already in the hotel but the whole while, I'm thinking, 'Where my family at? I don't know where they are. Are they hurt? Are they OK? ' I wasn't going to leave that city until I found out where all my people at. I just wasn't. When I got the phone call and found out that everybody was alright, I left."[6]

WAYBLACKMEMORIES.
RAVVA SPEAKS FROM THE 9TH WARD:

> The metal rails
> The threat of puncture,
> the loss of air
> The shards of glass,
> the cut of stories we hear
> when we listen,
> our past is littered with
> elegy Is punctuated
> by the still speaking

SILENCE, MEMORIES, BROKEN LEVEES AND
THE HEJIRA TO PHILLY

Silence. Memories. Destinies. From New Orleans to Philly. Long Journey. Trumpets still blowing. Louis Armstrong to Lee Morgan. Saints Go Marching in To Cornbread. Not yet Gabriel. Levees split memories and families. Jeremy reenters the jagged cipha: "I went to the levee because they say they'd carry us to the airport. They said to all of us, 'Go to the levee and they will come and get you.' And they took us to the airport. I arrived at the Louis Armstrong Airport in New Orleans, Tuesday Morning. They had one plane going out. They say it was going to near Memphis. They had a whole lot of people there so I couldn't get on that plane. So we had to wait for another plane. At the airport, they just said, 'Go where you can go and just get out of here.' They let us ride for free but we still had to go through security and everything." What happened next? "Man, I'm bout to tell you right now! So I kept asking the airline lady what was going on. She said she didn't know. So we got on another plane and we up in the air. I'm like, 'Where are we going? Are we staying Down South?' And they were like, 'Yeah. But we don't know where we going at, though we staying downsouf.' Then later on I asked the lady, 'What city we over?' She said, ' Atlanta.' I'm like, 'This where I need to be. Right here.' Lady said, 'We can't do that.' We watching a movie on the plane, *Mr. and Mrs. Smith*."[7]

WELCOME TO THE PHI: 'PRETTY LONG WAYS FROM HOME."

Fast speed. The marching band is playing as Billy Paul sings, " Me and Mrs. Jones" in Billy Penn's City. It's Holy Tuesday and they've got the day off. But where is the plane headed? Voice # 19 speaks: " The woman on the plane said, 'Well, they figured out they going to Philadelphia now.' I said, 'That's a pretty long ways from home.' I wanted to stay downsouth cause I would've had better reach of my family. Next thing I know, I'm in Philly. I don't even know the Mayor. When I got to the airport they had the Mayor out there. They had all kinds of people welcoming us to Philadelphia. They must have known I was coming. There were twenty-eight people from New Orleans on that flight. I was surprised when they greeted us at the airport but at the same time I was kinda mad because I thought I was going to stay down south. But the people in Philadelphia welcome me and been nice to me. The first night in Philly was a little cold."[8]

THE ARRIVANTS FROM JEFFERSON PARISH, MAGNOLIA PROJECTS AND ST. B'NARD

Jeremy Collier continues his narrative of new beginnings: " I arrived here Tuesday. We went to Wanamaker School and they fed us. Man, they had good food. Some roast beef sandwiches, sprite and potato chips. That made a good little meal. We got a chance to get a hot bath, lay down and rest. We hadn't had lights in several days. We didn't have no water on or nothing after Katrina hit New Orleans. I mean, this was a blessing for us because we could have been dead right now. When I left, over 2,000 people had died. And they could be some of my family. But I talked to my Mama and my close family. She's in Atlanta. She left before the storm. We have a lot of hurricanes down there but none of them were this bad. We'd had hurricanes come and go but it was always another day the next day. The newscaster warned us late. They could have been told us. I started out from there by myself. See, I lived in Jefferson Parish on Sizeler Street. They told us, 'You got to evacuate. You can't stay here because they ain't going to cut on the lights or the water in three months.' I saw all my neighbors going. So I went to the levee." Jeremy's voice trails off as reflects, " I don't know. I got hold of my Mama in Atlanta. She told me to do my best to get back down to Atlanta."[9]

PHILLY'S HIP HOP COMMUNITY
PROVIDES CRUCIAL SUPPORT

In cities all over the world, people came together to aid the survivors of Hurricane Katrina and the disastrous aftermath. A number of Philadelphia artists came together at the Robin Hood Dell East to participate in a Project Brotherly Love Benefit Concert spearheaded by members of Philly's burgeoning Hip Hop community. This event was coordinated by Charles "Charlie Mack" Alston in an effort to raise funds to assist those who came to Philadelphia following Hurricane Katrina. Among the artists and other members of the leisure time industry present were: Allen Iverson, Ms. Jade, Young Gunz, Freeway, Peedi Crakk, Musiq, Tye Tribett & Greater Anointing Gospel Praise Aggregation, Floetry, Hansoul and Jill Scott.

MUSIQ AND IVERSON WELCOME
FAMILIES FROM LOUISIANA

Conversations with many of the outstanding artists in attendance revealed their unusually keen and caring insight into the plight of those many thousands gone from New Orleans, Southern Mississippi and Alabama. When asked about the significance of this coming together for a common cause, the noted musician Musiq, explains: " I think this activity today is important because it shows folks that no matter where on the totem pole you may stand, you can always do a little bit to help. Nobody is too far gone that they can't see the needs of the people. This is not a political ploy. This is for real. Any little bit that you can do is needed. I was answering phones yesterday in New York City. Today, I'm in Philly doing a benefit for the people in Louisiana. In the coming days, I'm going to be doing something else to aid in the cause."[10] Allen Iverson made a rare appearance at this benefit concert and he made it clear why he was there, "You have all the bad stuff that goes on in the world everyday. But there is a lot of good people out here. I just wanted to be a part of this thing. It's good for the world to see that we care about what's going on and that we have not forgotten. Everything is going to be alright. We got to just welcome them the right way. When people come here, we are going to just accept them and they are going to be part of our family." When we asked him why he came out this Saturday afternoon, a few days before leaving for Japan, Iverson says, "I just wanted to show my love. I go through a lot of hard times in my life but it's nothing like this. Just to be a part of this and for people to want me to be a part of this benefit concert, I feel blessed."[11]

FAMILIES THROWN ASUNDER,
SPIRITUAL SUPPORT NEEDED

Musiq describes his first reaction to Hurricane Katrina," When I first saw the scene in New Orleans, I said, ' Ah, that's messed up, because I know what it is like not to have anything. But this is a little bit more. These people had stuff but they got it taken away from them. These are people who spent their whole lives building up what they had and now with all of the water, it's all underwater. It's gone. You've got Mothers out there who have lost family members and are trying to find out where their children are; getting separated from their kids. You got Fathers up here who don't have the means to take care of their families. That's kinda crushing to a man's pride. You know what I mean? This requires more than just physical support. Sometimes, it requires spiritual support. That could be the very thing that enables a person to keep going. You've got ninety-year-old people that have the feeling, 'I'm on my way out so why even stick around?' You can let them know if you can't give money, even if you can't give clothes, even if you can't give food. Give some time."[12]

JILL SCOTT REMEMBERS NEW ORLEANS

Jill Scott picks up where Musiq leaves off. She states, " My first reaction on seeing that hurricane was shock. Still shocked because there was so much water. I know people were afraid. I mean, anything over 6 feet for me and I'm in a pool. I'm scared. So I was just shocked from the beginning. And then I became sad. Looking at the news, I became depressed. I'm looking around. I'm walking around in my clean home. I can shower if I want to and I have toilet paper if I need it. Then I became angry. Just pissed, because as the days went by here I am sitting on my couch, in my home and I'm seeing people still wading in water, with feces and dead bodies, insects biting their flesh. All of that. It made me so angry. Pissed is what I was and what I still am. I became even more angry because I'm looking and I'm waiting for someone to help these folks. I'm thinking, where is our government? We are always singing songs before a baseball game and a basketball game, holding our hands over our hearts. But if it's not reciprocal, what is it? What is this? I'm singing songs. And I'm standing up every time I see a flag. I'm doing my thing. You know, 'American. Patriotic. Whatever.' People are outraged around the world because America is on its high horse. Other countries are looking and saying, 'Oh God. They really don't' have it together at all."[13]

Wayblackmemories. Jill Scott, " My first memory of New Orleans was The Essence Fest. First, I did one of the Super Lounges. I hosted a show with

Doug E. Fresh. And Eric Benet performed that year. The following year I was on the main stage. . . I just remember the music and having some really good food. I had some great fish out there." When asked what she would say to her many fans in Philadelphia and beyond who want to do something in support of the hurricane evacuees, Jill pauses for a moment, reflects and says, "Don't listen to me. Listen to your heart. We are all human beings and you have to take a look at what you have. Really pay attention to it."[14]

MESSAGE TO QUESTLOVE:
'I'M OUT HERE. CAN YOU HELP ME?'

Reflecting on her experiences and her family's expectations as she came to consciousness in North Philly, Jill notes, "I'm going to tell you right now, nothing makes me more upset than when I ride through North Philly and I see people standing on the corner and sitting on the steps and there is a whole heap of garbage around them. That is your community! That really angers me. I didn't do that. My mother wouldn't allow that. You've got to sweep the porch and the home. We are expecting someone to come along and clean up the neighborhood for us, whether it is garbage or whether it is violence. When it comes to those impacted by Katrina, look around at what you have and share. The blessings will come back to you ten fold. First, I looked around my house. I got all the extra tooth brushes, all the tooth brushes, all the tooth paste I had for guests, put that in a box. Do you know how much stuff you get as a celebrity? People give you stuff all the time. I went through all of that stuff. I put those things in a box and sent it out to Detroit. My girlfriend is a teacher in Detroit and people were coming from New Orleans to Detroit. So I sent those boxes to her in Detroit because I knew it would get into the hands of those who actually need it. Shoes. I'm a shoes fool. I have a lot of shoes, a lot of bags, a lot of clothes. I boxed those up and sent them out. I went out to Target and brought anything I thought people might need and sent it along to the people who needed it. I did SOS with BET last night and I'll also be with the Roots and Friends at the Kimmel Center. They are doing a benefit concert to help this young band from New Orleans who sent a message to Questlove saying, ' I'm out here. Can you help me'?"[15]

MUSIC HELPS PEOPLE SURVIVE THE STORM SURGE

Jill concludes with words about the importance of music in times like these: "Music can take you on vacation. It can make you disappear from what is happening in your life for just a moment. It can help you to get it together and help you cry if you need to. Music helps you experience the humanity again. Not the devastation. Not the fear. . . I will tell anybody who is still there, anybody who just left- SURVIVE."[16]

Jarrett Jackson, a native of New Orleans, recent Howard University graduate and music producer with Floetry, reflects on the importance of support provided by rap artists and other musicians to Katrina evacuees: " This Katrina Relief Benefit at Dell East today means everything to me being that I was born and raised in New Orleans, Louisiana. That's my life. It hits home real hard. I'm from the 13th ward. That's Uptown, Milan and Magnolia Street. I've been away for a minute going to school but it hits home because its real. It's unreal to people like us because everything we knew and grew up on is kinda washed away. It takes this type of event to happen to see and feel the love that everybody else is showing. I'm just blessed. And I continue to say my prayers. . . I was in Philadelphia when I saw it happen. This hurricane is basically the myth that we've heard all of our lives, that one bad hurricane would just have us under water."[17]

UNDER WATER SEARCH FOR YEMANGA

Faces move in and out of sight. Communing with Yemanga. She is the goddess of the sea. Dark nights turn into even more darkness. Dead bodies float down familiar/familial streets. Where is hoooomme??? How can the family be whole when there are so many floating bodies. Under Water. Whose father is missing? Where is Old Man Glapion. He'd gone to prayer meeting at the church. Never returned home. Did Hakim attend classes at the University of Islam today? Southern University's side door is half closed. The lights in the temple at Ilhadan are off. What day is this? I can still hear Louis Nelson's trombone from afar and the Banjo player did not march in this year's Black Indian parade. Floats are under water. Beneath the land mass where it is only dark. Katrina began to form over the Bahamas and it moved across southern Florida with the speed of a West African harmattan. Reconnecting the ancestors who'd been scattered all over the new world. But they are not alone. Yemanga's sons and daughters are never alone. Even as the angry tide brushes against the shores of this strange strange land, a voice cries out: "Fly Home."

Bodies piled as high as the Empire State building. Misery is even higher. Black people been knowing this tragedy, been living its reality. Levees in their lives had already been broken before those levees separated Lake Pontchatrain from New Orleans. Charles warned of an impending doom. Mardi Gras without the djembe players. Playas all moved to Houston. Levees washing it all under water. But in Atlanta the Blood Nation is reassembling, resuscitating memory and longing for another day in New Orleans. For the moment they've got their new Marta cards with the smart chip fully embedded and flashing the news to headquarters. Issued by the central office, they now can be tracked on their mission. Doing it underground. Five Point is their destination. But there is a new reality for those who have come to live in the ATL. Imminent clashes between the street marauders and snow men. Blue jackets symbolize cryptic crip walkers. Moonwalking and moonshining. Destinies. Memories and the motion of history. Flying Home. Ndong's novel captivated so much of what we did not yet see. Sea waves moving through our lives. Nawleeeeeeeeeeeeeeenssssssss.

LATE LIKE FEMA

"I've never been late like FEMA about being hip to the streets and knowing what's going on around me." . . . E-40 Hailing and Reigning from The Bay/ Yay in Cali.[18]

Africa's children lying and dying in their feces. Not even a proper burial. The Gods are not pleased. I don't know why she keeps talking about olives. Olive trees. Olive Fruits. Olive oil for those lying sick in the streets of New Orleans. Olive fatigues for the Souljahs. What happened under water? Were those cruise ships parked offshore made of olive wood? Levees broken and so are memories. A thousand memories were condensed into a giant singular memory. But who remembers the enslaved Africans who predicted a mighty wind. Blowing incessantly and without cease. Praying. Knowing. Being. Doing. Teaching. They are survivors. Ravensbruck to Angola. Bodies lie in front of sinking camps. Marshland in Mississippi. But who remembers the 1927 Flood when Africans were pushed further down into the 9th ward. Moving to higher ground. No way. And which city did FEMA officials visit? Where were the dirt men?

YOU DOWN WITH OPP?

Are you down with OPP? OPP is Orleans Parish Prison where the mostly black population of 7,000 are making room for those pushed into this new domain as a result of a collapsed judicial system. No lights and no water. Hospitals still closed. Schools unable to open. Prisoners abandoned in their cells with water all around them. Who will speak for those buried in silence. Juvenile's video captures the mode and motion of this historic moment in his native land. David Banner rhymes about this catastrophe and raises money for its survivors.

Numerous interviews were conducted with the survivors of Hurricane Katrina, city planners, FEMA officials, sociologists, folklorists, musicians, painters, preachers, politicians and a host of others familiar with what happened. In an effort to personalize Hurricane Katrina survivor's stories were chosen to have them say it in their own words. Finally, these voices were seldom heard as members of the media, the political establishment and the business community, joined other experts in telling their stories. Our intent in presenting this visual and written text is to deepen our historical understanding of Hurricane Katrina and the people who survived it. Thousands of people are miles and miles from home. All they have are motions, memories and a will to survive.

NOTES

1. "When government fails—the pathetic official response to Katrina has shocked the world. How will it change America?" Editorial, The Economist, September 9, 2005, p. 4.

2. Jeremy Collier, Unpublished interview by James G. Spady, August, 2005.

3. John Fernandez, Unpublished interview by James G. Spady, August, 2005.

4. Edward Allen, Unpublished interview by James G. Spady, August, 2005.

5. Ibid.

6. Ibid.

7. Jeremy Collier, Unpublished interview by James G. Spady, August, 2005.

8. Edward Allen, Unpublished Interview by James G. Spady, August, 2005.

9. Jeremy Collier, Unpublished interview by James G. Spady, August, 2005.

10. Musiq Soulchild, Unpublished interview by James G. Spady, August, 2005.

11. Allen Iverson, Unpublished interview by James G. Spady, August, 2005.

12. Musiq Soulchild, Unpublished interview by James G. Spady, August, 2005.

13. Jill Scott, Unpublished interview by James G. Spady, August, 2005.

14. Ibid.

15. Ibid.

16. Ibid.

17. Jarret Jackson, Unpublished interview by James G. Spady, August, 2005.

18. Corey Bloom, "The Ambassador of the Bay: E-40 the Artist, the Entrepreneur, and the Man," Synthesis, January, February 2006, 62–65.

And Before I'll be a slave, I'll be buried in my grave!

Chapter Two

From Refugee Camps to the City of the Dead: Poverty in the Middle East

Andrew Exum

Every now and then I wonder
How good things would be if we didn't have to suffer
But when I look around
I can't help but get down
'cause everything I see—is paining me

—*"Souls" Rob Murat*

Smiling broadly, Hoda invites me into her home and offers me tea. As with most Egyptians, Hoda is welcoming and courteous toward foreigners. But because Hoda's home is in itself a kind of tourist attraction, she—more than other Egyptians—is used to curious Western visitors. Hoda does not live in a famous mansion or tourist attraction you can find on a map, however. Hoda lives in a *tomb*—a crypt where others, unrelated to Hoda, are buried.

In Cairo, on the east side of the Nile, thousands of Egyptians have for centuries lived in what the Egyptians call the *Qarafa*, or "cemetery." Known by foreigners as the City of the Dead, the area is a vast necropolis located in the middle of the city. The tombs and crypts resemble the giant aboveground cemeteries in New Orleans, only each of the tombs is located within an enclosed space, usually with a room or two attached for visiting relatives. In days past, it was fairly common for relatives to visit their ancestors and then stay the night.

But Cairo is a large city, home to more than 16 million people. The housing crunch here is one that has been felt since almost the establishment of the city in 972 but has gathered pace over the past 100 years as millions of peasants have flocked to the city from the countryside in search of work or just trying to escape the areas periodically ravaged by the last century's wars.

As a Westerner, the City of the Dead strikes me first and foremost as an example of abject poverty. Children running around without clothes or shoes in the dirt streets, emaciated chickens living in makeshift pens, refuse piled high on the corners—these are the same images I remember from the slums of Port-au-Prince or from rural Afghanistan.

But for the Egyptians—and those who live within the Qarafa especially—the City of the Dead is nothing too remarkable. There is, if anything, a little curiosity toward the Westerners and others who have turned the dirt streets and crypts into a tourist attraction. For the natives of Cairo, the City of the Dead is just another neighborhood—and one in which stores, schools, and cafes have sprung up around the crypts and tombs in which the residents live.

This difference in opinion—the difference between what I, as an American, consider poverty and what my Egyptian peers see—started me thinking about several problems we as Westerners face when thinking about poverty on the global scale. "Poor" and "poverty," for a start, are words that come burdened with distinctly Western, industrialized definitions—and also serve as labels that we can slap onto whatever situations or people we see fit. There is a complicated power dynamic at work here, and one in which the powerful (the "developed" world) names and labels the weak, telling the weak exactly what he or she is. This dynamic is—in places like Egypt—often further complicated by the colonial legacies and experiences endured by the country in question.

But I don't mean to suggest that we start thinking about poverty issues in some post-modern mindset that refuses to let us use the label "poverty" for fear of offending some unspoken post-colonial psyche. After all, those of us who have seen truly wretched poverty know all too well what we're looking at when it stares us in the face. It could also go without being said that the fight against global poverty and for health and human rights is far too important and grave to let semantic games get in the way of whom we help and don't help. I *do* mean to suggest, however, that something is missing from the way we often think about and speak of the world's poor: the voices of the poor themselves. In every community I have visited—rich and poor, Western and Oriental—every community has different shared experiences that shape the way they think about themselves and their condition. While this may read like a painfully obvious observation, it's one at which I have arrived only after much travel and experiences of my own.

Growing up in East Tennessee, it seemed reasonable enough for the poor to be grouped into just two different communities. As a child, for example, I was vaguely aware of the *urban* poor. I say "vaguely" because while I knew they existed, I had only really seen them on television. They were black (as I learned from TV), lived in places like New York City and Philadelphia, and looked, acted, and spoke in ways very different from the ways in which my family and I did. The urban poor who inhabited my hometown of Chattanooga, of course, were something different. Though they too were mostly black and lived in economically depressed areas that a native of the South Bronx would find familiar, I did not consider them to be poor. They just *were*, and what they were was *normal*. I just assumed, riding in my mother's station wagon through urban Chattanooga, that the men and women I saw sitting on stoops smoking cigarettes were perfectly happy doing so. And just as my father grew up in Chattanooga in the 1950s thinking racial segregation was perfectly normal, so too did I grow up in the 1980s thinking there was nothing wrong with the way that so many African-Americans lived in my hometown. After all, most of my black friends—I, being a member of the first generation of white southerners to really *have* black friends—were middle class like me. I just assumed all other black people enjoyed similar levels of comfort.

The rural poor—the other category I recognized—were not so easy to dismiss or consider "normal." For one, they looked like me and spoke in the same nasal, East Tennessee accent. For another, their communities were not too far from the neighborhoods where I grew up. Driving through the small mountain communities in East Tennessee and North Georgia, I didn't need a dictionary to tell me that *this* was what poor meant, as I passed a family living in a rundown trailer home in what seemed like the middle of the wilderness. My father, a man of some importance and fame in the region, would often stop and talk to the men if we happened to be in the area. I, meanwhile, stared at the dirty and rough-speaking kids as if I had been put onto another planet. Who *were* these people?

So for me, there were two communities of poor: one rural and one urban, one real and one imagined. One community I knew from the rural areas of Tennessee, and one I knew from their representations on television and in movies. And all of this made poverty, for me, a black and white issue—quite literally, in fact. On the one hand, I could see the black urban poor on my television set. And on the other hand, I could see and interact with the rural white poor living just outside my hometown.

Later, however, as I grew up, I began to travel—not just outside of Tennessee but also through the world. My first brush with a global community of poor was in Haiti, where I helped build a school as part of a church mission. These people lived in conditions unlike anything I had ever seen, and I struggled to fit them into my black and white view of poverty despite the fact that their skin color was, in fact, black. I had been in college, in Philadelphia, for a year now and had by this point discovered the fact that my southern accent and vernacular actually had more in common with the poorer black residents of West Philadelphia than they did with the speech patterns of any of my boarding school-educated white peers at the University of Pennsylvania.

What's more, the poor black residents of Philadelphia had experienced a collective narrative that I had not experienced but nonetheless found familiar as part of a common American narrative. These Haitians, by contrast, had experiences *completely* different from my own. Once again, I had the feeling that I had landed on another planet. I simply did not possess the faculty to understand anything about the lives the Haitians lived in what were, for me, unimaginable conditions.

This feeling—that of being a visitor from some different, far-off world— was one that I would experience repeatedly over the coming years. After college, I served as an officer in the U.S. Army, and from the September 11th attacks until the time I left the army in 2004, I deployed to Kuwait, Afghanistan, Iraq, and Afghanistan again. If while in Haiti I had considered myself a bit of a space traveler, in Afghanistan I felt this even more strongly. It's not hard too understand why, either. Over the course of my duties during my first tour there, I would often conduct combat missions in Southeast Afghanistan that required me to travel, by helicopter, from the secure former Soviet base north of the capital and over several hundred miles of mountainous terrain to the area of operations.

On the way there and back, I would sit at the back of the helicopter and look out onto the foreign landscape that rushed by below my feet. The people of eastern Afghanistan live, predominantly, in small huts and buildings made from stone, clay, and mud. Outside of the capital city, there was, in 2002, very little electricity. And for me, whizzing by the villages at over 100 miles and hour, all I could see of them were what I considered to be their wretched conditions of living. Surely humans—belonging to the same animal species as I did—didn't live in those conditions, did they? Even when I did come into actually human contact with the Afghanis, I'm sure *I* was the one who looked like the alien. I, after all, was invariably loaded down with 60 pounds of gear including helmet, body armor, and assorted weaponry.

Throughout my time in the army, there was always that wall of separation— a wall of incomprehension between me, on one side, and the indigenous peoples with whom I interacted on the other. Because I could not speak their languages, didn't know their customs, and had only traveled to their counties by order of the President of the United States, I had a tough time putting myself in the place of the human beings I encountered.

Leaving the army in 2004, however, I moved to Beirut, Lebanon and began graduate school there. For me, this was the first time I had actually lived outside the country on a long-term basis. Something happens when you *live* someplace as opposed to when you *travel* there. When you travel, it is easy to think of yourself—as I had in Haiti, in Iraq, in Afghanistan—as a visitor from another planet. And when confronted with things foreign—be they languages, cultures, or poverty—it's easy enough to quickly dismiss such things as aberrations, things that will go away in a relatively short period of time. When you live someplace, however, you are forced to really come to terms with the environment in which you are living. You are also forced to interact with the people among whom you are living. This happened for me as I made my home in the Middle East.

Lebanon is a unique country in both the Middle East and in the world at large. Whereas countries like Saudi Arabia or Jordan are more or less heterogeneous as far as their populations are concerned—both of these countries being predominantly Arab and Muslim—Lebanon is the home to many different faiths and peoples. Even other countries in the Arab world that are diverse in terms of religious groups and ethnicities—such as Iraq or even Egypt with its large Coptic Christian population—cannot come close to the diversity of Lebanon. Lebanon is home to 19 officially recognized religious sects, and due to the confessional nature of its politics, each of these sects has a political voice. There are Sunni Muslims, Shia Muslims, Maronite Christians, Armenian Christians, Greek Orthodox Christians, Druze and an assortment of other religious and ethnic groups. Until the Lebanese Civil War and Israel's two invasions of the country, there was even a small but thriving Jewish community.

One group, however, has never found a voice in Lebanon's confessional system: the Palestinian refugees, estimated at 373,440 by the United Nations Relief and Works Agency (UNRWA) in 1999. Considering the relatively small size of Lebanon (pop. 3.8 million), the Palestinian refugees make up a large percentage of the people living in the country today. But unlike in Syria or in Jordan—two other countries where large numbers of Palestinian refugees fled after the establishment of the state of Israel in 1948—in Lebanon the Palestinians enjoy very few rights. Why?

The answers lie in the complex political power-sharing arrangements between Lebanon's sects. According to a 1933 census that established the percentages of Muslims and Christians in the country, each sect is allowed a certain number of parliamentarians and political positions within the Lebanese government. Christians are, as far as the government is concerned, still a majority in Lebanon. On the ground, however, this is no longer the case—and may not have even been the case at the time of the dubious 1933 census. Today in Lebanon, Muslims make up approximately 60 percent of the population according to the most recent CIA World Fact Book. And some political analysts estimate that the exploding Shia Muslim population alone tops over 45 percent of the overall population. All this makes Lebanon's Christians—traditionally among the country's socio-economic over-class—very nervous. The 15-year Lebanese Civil War, which began in 1975, was largely fought as the result of long-simmering tensions between Lebanon's sects. It was also fought in large part due to the increasingly vocal and powerful Palestinians presence in Lebanon, which angered the Maronite Christian parties especially. What began as tit-for-tat massacres between Maronite and Palestinian militias in the 1970s eventually grew into a full-scale global crisis that involved all the world's major powers and sent serious repercussions reverberating through the region for over a decade.

In one of the more horrific episodes of the war, Christian militias—aided and abetted by the occupying Israeli army—killed over a thousand Palestinian civilians in the infamous Sabra and Chatilla massacres of 1982. The resulting political shock waves in Israel led to then-Defense Minister Ariel Sharon losing his job and being cast into the political wilderness for the next 18 years. The Palestinians, meanwhile, still for the most part live in the same horrid refugee camps today as they did then. Today, 56 percent of the Palestinians in Lebanon live in the refugee camps that are officially administered by UNRWA but are often, in effect, lawless and shocking to the eye of a Western observer.

In Jordan, Palestinian refugees have been given citizenship and, in theory, enjoy equal rights alongside the native Jordanians. Jordan, however, is a monarchy in which there are not so much *citizens* as there are subjects of the king. Lebanon, flawed though it may be, is an actual democracy. And if Lebanon were to make the largely Sunni Muslim Palestinians refugees citizens, the entire confessional balance keeping the country from descending into another civil war would be thrown into disarray.

So the Palestinians remain in limbo. They enjoy no real legal rights and are considered "visitors" to Lebanon—even though many of them were born in Lebanon and have lived in the country for over 40 years. They must obtain a work permit in order to seek employment, and in reality the kinds of jobs available to them are limited for fear they will take well-paying jobs from the Lebanese. They cannot vote, are entitled to no social security (despite having to make these payments), and are prohibited from constructing any buildings in their camps that could be considered "permanent." After 50 years, it does not take a first-person visit to imagine the wretched conditions in these camps.

I do not mention the Palestinian refugees in Lebanon, though, as an argument about Israel, the peace process, or even human rights in the Middle East. Rather, I mention Lebanon's Palestinians because of the stark contrast between them on the one hand and the Egyptians in the City of the Dead on the other. For the most part, the Egyptians living in the City of the Dead do not consider themselves to be living in great poverty. Despite their condition, after all, they are better off than many others in Egypt—and they know this. For while the Egyptians are proud of saying that they descend from "the Pharaohs," the reality is less glamorous. As one of my Lebanese friends puts it, "Only one of them was the Pharaoh—the rest were slaves."

In other words, Egypt has always had a large lower class with a small upper class—and a very large gap between the two with almost no middle class to speak of. If the truth be told, very little has changed since the days of the Pharaohs. And so the Egyptians with whom I spoke in the City of the Dead, though conscious that they did not have as much wealth as others, were not as discontent as an American—with our sense of entitlement that goes along with being a citizen in the midst of the world's largest economy—might have been had he or she been in a similar situation.

The Palestinian refugees in Lebanon, however, are a people very conscious of—and very bitter about—their condition. The refugees themselves come in two groups: 1948 refugees and 1967 refugees. The 1967 refugees fled after the Israeli occupation of the West Bank and the Gaza Strip following the 1967 War. And while they do not have as many rights as do the 1948 refugees in Lebanon, they *do* have a greater chance of returning to their homes someday when a final settlement is arrived at between the Palestinian Authority and Israel. The 1948 refugees, on the other hand, are in a much different situation. For them, the often-mentioned "right to return"—that is, the right to return to the homes and villages they fled in 1948—is but a far-off dream. Somewhat understandably, Israel has consistently stated that they will not allow any unlimited right to return as it would completely wreck Israel's society and demographics. And in the most recent talks between the Palestinian Authority and Israel, it has appeared as if the "right to return" is no longer even on the table for discussion. All of which leads a friend of mine, Maha, a Palestinian refugee, to say the following:

> "Now, I'm a 1948 refugee though I was born in Lebanon. My grandparents came here, and I still have family living in the camps near Saida [Sidon]. I only have a Palestinian identification card. I don't have a passport, I can't hold but a certain number of jobs, and because my family comes from what even the United Nations says is legal Israel, my family can't ever go back. But also, we can't leave. Basically, I'm f****d."

At least two thirds of my conversations with Maha and other Palestinian friends, it's worth noting, are in English—not Arabic. Like many Palestinian refugees, Maha is college-educated and speaks English fluently. Many Palestinians in Lebanon also speak French (like so many Lebanese), and still more learn German in the hopes of leaving to attend university in Europe. Many more have used their education to escape the camps and find paying jobs in the UN or elsewhere. So unlike the Egyptians living in the City of the Dead, with their awful schools and little concept of what life is like outside Egypt, the Palestinians are all too aware of what life is like outside of Lebanon. They can read the newspapers, they watch the news, and many have even been able to travel outside Lebanon's borders. They are a people, as I mentioned earlier, entirely conscious of their condition.

As I talk to Palestinian friends in Lebanon or with the Egyptians living in the City of the Dead, I don't—as you might expect—wonder what it would be like if others in America or Europe could hear their stories. What really makes me curious is what a conversation would be like *between* them. If a Palestinian from Lebanon and an Egyptian from the City of the Dead had a conversation, what about the other's condition would they find familiar? What would they find different? Is there such a thing as a shared experience of poverty? Could the poor of Appalachia see themselves in the people living in the City of the Dead, caught in an endless cycle of poverty? Could African-Americans from New Orleans' Ninth Ward recognize their own experiences in those of the Palestinians of Beirut?

As much as I would like to say yes, I instead believe that if you were to transplant a Palestinian into East Tennessee or a poor African-American from North Philadelphia into the City of the Dead, their experience would be something akin to what I felt so long ago in Haiti: the experience of being a space traveler dropped into a world completely foreign. And that, maybe, is the lesson in all this: that there is no such thing as a shared experience called "poverty."

Each group—rich or poor, Western or Oriental—has its own collective narrative. And to address the needs of any group, you must first address that narrative. Just as the old maxim "all politics is local" is proven time and time again, so too is it fact that all poverty is local. The experiences and needs of the Palestinians of Lebanon are radically different from the Palestinians of Jordan—much less the Egyptians in Cairo's City of the Dead. Recognizing this, however, might well be the easy part. Much more difficult would be to actually addressing those needs. This requires actually listening to and interacting with the poor—in their own individual communities. That also means learning new languages, learning new customs, and generally removing ourselves from the comfort zone from which we normally operate in the West and in America in particular. The end result, of course, means definitions for "poverty" and "poor" much different from what we define them as today. Different, yes, but, in the end, also more human.

Chapter Three

Come and See: A Theology of the Poor

Debbie Little-Wyman

> *We don't live plush*
> *We ain't got much*
> *But that don't mean a thing*
> *'cause we got soul—soul—soul!*

> —*"Souls" Rob Murat*

I cannot write *about* theology of the poor. But I can tell some stories about our poorest people in Boston and how they talk about God. I should say that my understanding of the "theology of the poor" is just mine, from my experiences and through my eyes and ears. I am not poor myself. I am a white middle-class woman who worked for nearly 30 years in publications and management. At midlife, I felt the tug to get out and meet folks on the park benches to see if there was anything I could offer and to learn about God from the people I feel Jesus sends us to. I wanted to learn about, and to do my part in the world, to get closer to what Jesus is doing and saying.

I fell in love with the understanding of God and the church and Jesus and the work of the people described by liberation theology. What made the most sense was their idea that the Christian life is not an abstraction. I learned that the poor can lead us into the shadow and depth and revelation of God who is present in the nooks and crannies, where God is *desired* and *sought* out of necessity. Even a white middle–class, Brand-X woman could seek salvation by a quest into the God of the oppressed expressed by others revealing my own poverty.

Of course, no one is "the poor" or "the homeless." Speaking of "the poor" is one way we either romanticize or stigmatize the majority of people on our planet-our neighbors-whom God clearly calls us to love not abstractly, but in

a concrete way. It does not seem honest to generalize. "Do not put meaning on it" my spiritual director admonishes me when I'm tempted to "understand" something. Hence I'll tell you some stories.

MY EXPERIENCE IN THE STREETS

At forty-five, I went to seminary and at fifty was ordained an Episcopal priest. The day after I was ordained, I put on a knapsack full of socks, string, a first-aid kit, meal and shelter lists, a prayer book, stole, healing oil, AA meeting lists, lip balm, and peanut butter and jelly sandwiches. I took to the streets. I still remember that first day. I stopped at the Cafe de Paris near the Ritz Hotel in Boston, bought two cups of coffee, and walked across the street to Boston Public Garden. I looked around for someone on a bench who "looked homeless." I spotted a man with a few paper bags, went over, and sat down. I had no idea what I should say. I handed him one of the cups of coffee. He took it, and looked at me. "So, how are you doing today?" he asked. In my first five minutes of "street ministry," I had learned who is ministering to whom.

A few weeks later, I asked Mary—who was sitting with all her things at her usual spot by a big church fountain-how she was doing. "I'm fine," she said. "God woke me up this morning." I never had that thought and certainly not after spending a night in a Back Bay alley. Jesus was right. Go to the poor to learn about God. Mary does not have an alarm clock, breakfast, a roof over her head, a job, a telephone call to make, or any of the protective layers that I am so anxious to offer her. But Mary has God Here is a woman in so much pain she has not gone inside anywhere for anything in at least twenty years. But Mary's terrors do not derive from lack of intimacy with God.

One miserable night, I was leaving a meeting downtown. Some cookies and donuts were left over so I decided to go up to Boston Common to see if anyone was around and hungry. It was pouring rain. Here, I ran into Sam on one of the benches. He asked if we could pray. "God, I know you are up there," he began, "but down here, things are real bad. I cannot stop drinking. But tonight, I am not praying for myself. A few days ago, my friend Fred died right over there." He pointed to the fountain in front of him. "When I found him, his shoes were missing. His hat was gone. He always wore his hat. These streets have turned to hell. We need you, God. I have lived on these streets for years. I do not have any money, but I will beg money for my brother if he needs it and I do not have it. I wish I had known Fred was in trouble. We have got to watch out for each other. God, help us." Sam did not go to any seminary. He is not an outreach worker. But Sam loves his neighbor and is on speaking terms with God. Even drunk and soaked to the bone, Sam knows God and directs himself to justice and righteousness. He may have as much trouble as any of us acting out that love every day, but he is close to the heartbeat.

DOING GOOD IS A HUSTLE

One morning in the early months, I got "The Question" I had dreaded since my first day of street ministry. "Why are you talking to me?" Jack asked from his panhandling post in front of a fancy jewelry store. I stammered out something like, "Just trying to be helpful." Jack—I had yet to learn that he is smarter than I—leaned against the window full of gold watches and said to me in the kindest way, "Doing good is a hustle, too, you know" Jack asks questions and expects the truth. Doing good is a hustle unless we get honest, confess our contradictions, and take care of ourselves so we do not spill out all over the people we want to care for and learn from. Being with poor people transforms us. That's a major way God's work and desire happens on earth.

We associate a kind of listening with Jesus and view it as integral to his healing powers. I have observed and am the recipient of that kind of listening all day long. A man named Luke has been homeless for five years now, having lost his apartment and his job due to what he names "injustices." He will sit for hours listening to Tommy, or Dusty Don, or any of a number of homeless men and women whom many of us find hard to listen to for even ten minutes. On a freezing night, Alex will search the Common for people too drunk to find their own way to a shelter. He will tie them to himself with a long rope, and pull them down the street to a warm place. It is important not to sentimentalize homeless people, but many are unaccountably generous.

Ernie always wants me to pray for his pal Sam who is dying in the blankets next to his under one of the bridges. Tom, who panhandles in front of a downtown church, says he always prays for the people who, he says, "look down on me." Roger and Bob, when I handed them blankets one snowy night asked me whom they could pray for. Moses always tells me God is taking care of him. "I know I cannot take care of myself. I just hope I do not keep God so busy other people get forgotten."

A block from St. Paul's Cathedral, Dave sits on the sidewalk upon folded cardboard with a cup. It is his daylight routine and a ministry. Back a year or so ago, when I first met Dave, I asked him, stupidly, "Why don't you go to the free meals?" and then "Could I bring you something from the soup kitchen?" "I like *whole* chicken," he replied. It was not hard for me to picture the way chicken comes at the Cathedral soup kitchen. "I do not need much," he said, "but I like to choose what I eat. *And I can't stand in a line."* With that sentence I understood that *none* of the "resources" I was so anxious to offer him would work. He was insisting on what he needed to be a free man. So, I sat down with him on the sidewalk. "Could you tell me about God?" I asked. "Oh, I know God," he responded. "I pray all day long. Mostly, I pray for all these poor people" as he swept his hand the length of Tremont Street. "They all look so sad, so lost, so busy . . . . They do not look like they know about Jesus. They do not know how much God loves them." I asked him to pray for me.

LEARNING ABOUT OURSELVES

One of the gifts of our homeless community is how much they teach us about ourselves. Being with people in such pain and proximity to the holy is excruciating and elating all at once. I often describe what I do as looking at my character defects all day long. I see my persistent need to fix people, to do something, *anything,* to assume my agenda should be the other person's. I learned the hard way in early interactions and still today, that my ongoing spiritual struggle is simply to *be* with people, to learn from them, to offer a suggestion if asked. I am not to expect or judge "results." Jesus asks "only" that we give wholeheartedly.

Each of us has our own path. Why should I sell the white, middle-class agenda, which creates its own miseries, to anyone? Such wisdom has come slowly to me, an I frequently forget it. Surely this is Jesus talking through the lives of the poor, calling us all to be simpler, to give without hope of return, not with disdain for people who make different choices, but to be openhearted and to love as God loves.

About a year and a half into my street ministry, on Christmas Eve, I decided to offer the Eucharist to people who spend the day in Boston's central train station. While I was reading the Christmas story, a gentleman spoke up. "My name is Joseph," he said through tears. "I wish I had been like this Joseph here," pointing to the text. "When my wife cheated on me, I hated her." I learned that evening about how immediate and concrete scripture is for people who have nothing between themselves and the good news. Joseph lives alone, just his bags, his meals, and God. Not to put meaning on that, but he is close enough to touch God. We have a lot to learn from him. Billy says, "I think every time I hear the Twenty-third Psalm the Holy Spirit is all around. And that is absolute proof to me that there is more than just people here-it is the Spirit, the living Spirit."

A few months after that train station service, I started a worship service outdoors in a public park, Boston Common. We have come together every Sunday since, where our gathering ranges between 100–150 people. We developed this service to offer church to people who cannot or will not come into buildings. Many homeless people have been frightened or shamed in churches. Others are concerned about their behavior or their dress or cannot stand enclosed places.

When non-homeless people began to hear about us and wanted to come, I was worried and protective. I did not want our folks to feel crowded or stared at or taken over. What I learned was that the homeless people were more ready than I to share our worship and their lives, thus welcoming the strangers from the suburbs. They speak of this as offering their "home" to others. They feel hopeful and want to connect with a world they have come to appreciate as hungry to learn from them.

A Native American started coming almost from the beginning, but not in our worship circle. Rather, he would sit on the steps of a church across the street. We would take him communion and a sandwich. He spoke very little. Once I asked who God is for him. Looking directly at me for the first time, with an incredulous look, he said, "Why, God is everywhere; God is in everything! I know *God* is with me," as if to underscore the tragic obvious, that otherwise he is alone.

BEYOND PERSONAL CONCERNS

Surprisingly, our homeless people are not simply concerned about their own life-threatening circumstances, although of course, food and shelter are crucial. Frances, who many homeless folks call "Mama," is one of the most faithful Christians. She has a booming voice for hymn singing and for whatever else is on her mind. She arrived one Sunday as we were reflecting on the story of Jesus healing the blind man, dropped her bags in the center of our circle, put her hands on her hips, and threw her head back for maximum volume. "I've heard all this gospel talk before," Frances said. "When is lunch?" Then she began the most powerful soul deep version of the hymn "I am Standing on Holy Ground."

Over and over, I experience the presence of the raising up of God's simple desires in the words and actions of our poorest people. They seem to pray more, be more grateful, worry about each other more, be more honest, and be clearer about who God is than most of the privileged people I know. Their access to truth and grace and their willingness to share themselves sets the table for everyone else. I thought I would hear a lot of anger toward God, but that was not the case. Perhaps expectations of God that lead to resentments and disappointment -are one more privilege of people who have enough to feel entitled to a "good life." Homeless people in America have always been blamed for their homelessness. What is true is that they do not fit into the usual molds of social success or control, as described by Kenneth Kusmer in *Down and Out* Nor do they always fit the mold with their theology and understanding of church and God (2002, 8).

THEOLOGICAL UNDERSTANDINGS

"I do not want to sound like I am off the wall, but the many times that I have invited God and Jesus to be here, He comes when He can. He does not come when I want Him to," Gary told me. "I notice Jesus more so because if you modernize the Bible it fits every one of us." Gary continued, "When I tell people my stories out on the streets, I try not to speak of the Bible, because I want my own credit. Jesus did his thing, and I do mine, and if they both seem to be the same, it's just one of those things."

Most people who live outside carry everything they own with them all day long. If they show you what they have in their bags, you will most often find a worn, obviously read, Bible. Our sisters and brothers who have nothing teach us who have everything about God, about life with Jesus, about church being a place where we tell the truth, break ourselves open, and allow ourselves to be held however well and badly humans do that. They teach us to claim our faith. Barbara stands in the middle of our circle singing "Amazing Grace" in that way only Barbara can, complete with tears running down her face. We who hear that want to run away. We have heard it before. We do not want pain, such pain, in the middle of our worship! Yet when she finishes, a woman from the suburbs who has everything her pain needs (medication, a psychiatrist, a church, a family, a home, education) will stand in the middle of that circle, and for the first time ever, tell us something she has been carrying alone about her own childhood. We all stand in awe and wonder in those moments.

One of our beloved, Alison, died on the grass of Common Cathedral. She was hugging her bottle, and she had our Common Cathedral cross around her neck. "Listen to me kid,"-it was Gary calling to console me "We all have a name out here because of you. We are all fighting the same system. The system wins; it takes away. But God takes care."

We privileged people have everything to learn from the poor. How do we go about doing that? It is easy to say and hard to do, but we need to do what we can to step out of our safety zones physically, emotionally, and spiritually.

Jose Comblin presses for what he calls "a true liberation" of theology. "Christian concepts of traditional theology have been distorted by the situation under Christendom." By "situation" he means domination, clericalism, and imperialism. "Everything has to be reexamined and reinterpreted-from the idea of God, to the theology of Christ, the church, grace and sin, the sacraments, and so forth" (1998, 213). We might ask: How can we step aside both to promote the freedom of our oppressed poor and to express and see God from their starting point? It is not enough to look at a theology of the poor from our usual social locations. The poor are free of the bonds and limitations of middle class understanding of theology because they are not included or beholden to it. Consequently, Jesus says it is much harder for the rich to enter the kingdom of God.

VISION DRIVING TO ACTION

Liberation theology tells us it is not enough for Christians to mean well. Our theology must include the vision of the poor, and this must drive us to action. In *Remember the Poor,* Joerg Rieger leads us to ask how has theology been part of the sin of growing imbalance and poverty in the third and first worlds? "At the beginning of the twenty-first century, a time when we have all gotten used to the victory of capitalism, poverty levels and other indicators of imbalance and injustice are increasing not only in certain parts of the 'third world' but in the 'first world' as well. There is still much left to be done (and to be undone). Theology needs to grasp its own role in this context." Rieger insists that this not be a matter of curiosity or superficial inclusion, but that we be driven by urgent necessity to achieve collaboration (1998, 224).

This collaboration, I would argue, should not simply be between theologians, clergy, and others who package words. It needs to happen at the level of life lived. The poor are the majority and must be listened and attended to. As Rieger argues, "without encounters with the repressed human other who is different, encounters with the divine Other are unlikely" (229). The poor have an angle of vision that we who are others, need. If we are to take drawing closer to listen and learn from the poor seriously, we must, as Rieger says, participate "in God's work of liberation already going on in both church and world and thus creating new forms of solidarity of rich and poor, oppressors and oppressed, and self and other. Here theology is reshaped. . . . The poor as teachers are able to expose hidden fault lines and to raise new questions that lead us beyond the current impasse" (222). What better vocation might we seek than our own particular response to Jesus' invitation, "Come and see."

Chapter Four

Tears in the Sudan

Brooke Beck

There's something 'bout the souls
Of my people
I'm talking bout the souls
Of my beautiful folks

—"Souls" Rob Murat

I find that this chapter you are about to read will be unique as my perspective and my heart's passion for the poor is for those souls who are in 3rd world developing nations. Growing up in middle class America, my life was relatively easy and sheltered. I entered the University of Pennsylvania as a BSN student in 1997 and was invited to participate in a study abroad program in Jersualem, Israel for the spring semester of junior year. That semester spent abroad ignited my heart for the plight, both physical and spiritual, for those living in poverty, oppression and suffering in lands beyond our borders that most Americans will only hear about on CNN. I knew that this passion that God gave me for the souls of His people abroad was from HIM, as your average single American girl would not voluntarily choose to live among the poorest of the poor.

My first real look at the poverty of those in developing nations came when I went to Afghanistan in 2003. Almost a year and a half after 9/11, the people of Afghanistan continued to live in fear, hopelessness and oppression. As a nurse, I have the privilege of being welcomed into most circles around the world regardless of race or religion simply because I provide medical care. For many people in Afghanistan, they have zero access to medical care. I was there in January, and in the mountains surrounding Kabul there were villages tucked away so high and far into the mountains that they had never had medical care.

These villages were mostly women and children and as we would come into the village they would cling to us. There homes were nothing more than mud huts, perhaps 10–12 people would sleep in a room no bigger than my bedroom at home. No heating, no electricity, no running water. Many of the women were widowed and they would share their stories of how the Taliban had burned their villages, killed their men and left them alone without food, medicines or any way to provide for their children. Even though there was snow on the ground, some of the children did not have socks and shoes, very few had a warm jacket. They pleaded with us to stay with them, however there was very little we could do except pray.

Many of the women still wear the burka. I don't know if they feel they can hide beneath the folds of the cloth, if this is the only way of life they know or why they continue to wear it. Perhaps it hides their pain and suffering, it shields them from the poverty of their daily lives. At that moment in Afghanistan I had a revelation from the Lord. The suffering that these Afghan people deal with on a day to day basis is a life of hopelessness, a life of mere survival. Their souls are crying out for someone to save them and without the knowledge of a Savior in Christ, it will be an eternity of suffering. How can we turn our backs on them and go back to a life filled with Venti Lattes from Starbucks, endless credit limits, fancy cars and surround sound HDTV? The disparity between life here in America and life over there was startling to me and I would never be the same.

This passion ignited my heart to quit a comfortable life and job and to move to live among those who were suffering to provide nourishment for their bodies and nourishment for their souls. I would travel and serve and work over the next couple of years in Iraq, the West Bank and the Darfur region of Sudan.

Darfur, Sudan was like nothing I had ever seen or experienced in my life. The poverty in Africa seems so daunting and overwhelming, I wonder if the world has given up on the entire continent. Ravaged by AIDS, Civil War, genocide, famine and political instability, the needs of the African nations have hit a climax and they have never been more clearly seen than in Sudan.

As I mentioned earlier, my profession as a pediatric nurse gives me access to some of the most remote areas of the world. Darfur, Sudan is one of those remote areas. I often wonder what the people on the plane to Khartoum thought of me. Perhaps a bit cynical, thinking I could never survive. Perhaps relieved, that someone from the West actually did care about the plight of the people. I myself wonder at times what finally pushed me to this part of the world.

When I disembarked from my UN WFP flight in El Geneina in West Darfur I thought I had woken up in a time warp. My thoughts started with, "You have got to be KIDDING me." No running water, sporadic electricity, no paved roads, drought and political unrest . . . I cried for an entire week wondering how in the world I would be able to survive. What is so amazing is that as humans we cannot survive in such a setting, it is only by the power of God and His grace that He equips us to do the work He has called us to.

I do not know how familiar you may be with the situation in Sudan. Sudan is unique as it is a mix of Arab/Middle Eastern culture and African culture. The language is Arabic but there are multiple tribal dialects spoken throughout the country. The southern part of Sudan is mainly Christian and African whereas the northern part, including the government, is Arab and Muslim.

In Darfur, there is tension and conflict between the Arab Muslim Janjaweed and the African Sudanese. The Janjaweed and the unrest that is ensuing have created a situation where more than 1–2 million Sudanese have been internally displaced, more are refugees and over 400,000 people have been killed in what has been declared by the United States as a genocide. This had created an increase in an already impoverished nation as I would see first hand.

I have never known the hopeless feeling of being thirsty. I don't mean thirsty after you have run a few miles, or thirsty because it is hot outside. I am talking thirsty to the point where you do not have access to water. I met women who would have to walk more than 4–6 hours ONE WAY to retrieve enough water for their families for one day. I remember a very specific day where there was not enough water in the village of Sanidadi. Women had been lining up since sunrise in hopes they would be able to fill their Water jericans with clean water. The local Janjaweed had ridden into the village and were pushing ahead of the women, flailing their weapons and allowing their horses to drink from the trough, littering the watering area with urine and feces, contaminating one of the few clean water sources for many miles. My heart burned with injustice, my translator hushed me as he pleaded with the militia men to please show grace, to allow the people working in the clinic to get clean water. Their response? They would rather have their horses have enough water than these women, including me. THESE were men? This was courage? Where was their soul? Their compassion? The conviction of right and wrong? My heart bled for the women and the children, who suffered day in and day out with no hope of the situation changing. They were so far removed from civilization, just trying to make it through the day out in the middle of the African desert.

Many days I wondered how they made it to the next day; how they survived the night and awoke afresh each morning . Surely the hand of God is upon the people, for in a state of poverty and starvation only He can sustain them. I remember going to the hut of a woman about 22 or 23-years-old and she was dying from some sort of immune disorder, perhaps HIV, perhaps Hepatitis. I remember this night very vividly because there was such a sense of unity across culture, across color, across socio-ecomonic standing. There I was with a physician from Alaska, my Sudanese translator and my driver. It was past sunset so of course there was no electricity in this village so my driver arranged our Land Rover to shine the headlights into the hut. I started an IV with the aid of a flashlight and used a rubber glove as a tourniquet and Muhammad my translator helped me with straw from the ceiling of the hut to rig the IV bag. The woman was burning with fever, she had diarrhea for more than 2 months, flies and insects were buzzing around her mouth and eyes and she was malnourished beyond what I thought was life. Yet as the doctor examined her, she had the strength to grasp my hand and her sunken eyes met mine and I remember the eerie feeling of her almost staring to my soul, searching for life. She looked as if she was pleading with me to save her: to save her soul and her body for she was helpless. I placed my hand on her forehead and prayed over her, spoke words of comfort that she couldn't understand the meaning of but could certainly feel the compassion I was pouring on her from my heart. Could I change her present circumstances? Slightly. Could I save her entire village from death and starvation. Probably not. Yet, did her family and relatives who had gathered silently outside of the tent wonder at these foreigners coming into their humble surroundings? Most definitely.

To reach people in compassion and love is far beyond dropping food or organizing a blanket distribution. It is kneeling down in the sand, meeting their most immediate need which is a cry of the soul for human love and compassion. To empathize with their situation and to love them despite what may seem is a chasm of difference that separates your lives. The people in Africa or in any of the 3rd world developing nations are more than statistics. I could have giving you the statistics of the number of starving people, the sky rocketing numbers of those suffering from HIV and AIDS, the number of orphans, the number of refugees but I have determined that numbers and stats don't change the behavior of those who hear them. We have enough stats and numbers to last a lifetime but there has been very little significant, sustainable change in the 3rd world to make a major difference in the life of the general population. Therefore I come with human stories of real people, with real faces and names whose souls are crying out for salvation in every sense of the word. These are people who will wait hours in the blazing African sun to be seen by a physician, who will walk for miles and miles in the middle of a miscarriage to get taken care of in the clinic, who will extend their very last morsel of food to me as a guest so that I feel welcome in their home. The people in these nations are just like you and me. They are mothers and wives, children, students, fathers, uncles. They desire peace within their borders, peace in their homes. The young men want to provide for their young families. Mothers desire education and success for their children. There are soccer games on the weekends, there are weddings, funerals, national celebrations. There is music, food, dancing and laughter. I have never been more warmly welcomed by people than I was in Africa and the Middle East. Funny how people with nothing materially can give so much to a person that I felt like the richest woman on earth when I was received into their homes. I wept like a child the day I left Africa. I feel like part of my heart will always remain there with the people. The richness of their culture, the sincerity of their hospitality has impacted me forever. How did I live my whole life in the comfort of my own home, in the seclusion of the life we create for ourselves in America? While the cell phones, email and the luxury of large homes and personal cars are convenient, we have missed out on some of the true richness of life that I see among the people in these countries. How can we ever live the same knowing that there are people on the other side of the world dying for lack of very basic needs such as clean water and medicine? Who will go to them? I was made rich in the midst of their poverty because of what I received from their culture and from sharing their lives. I will always go back to them for I cannot erase what has been imprinted upon my heart. Truly I love them. Their souls have touched my own soul and my heart breaks for the poverty of life they have been given to handle. May the mercy of the Lord rest upon them. May we who have been given much also return our blessings to those who have not. It is truly more blessed to give than to receive. My life has been blessed by living among these poor folk in a land so different from my own, and by people who are in their passions and souls our very brothers and sisters. What a privilege to live in their land and experience their life. I will never be the same and pray for God's blessing and truth to rain upon these lands in a mighty way.

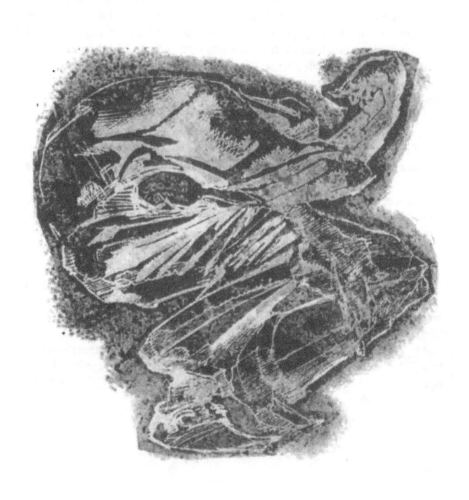

Chapter Five

America Goddamn: God and Hip Hop in an Age of War, Terror and Dread

Erik Williams

But we hustle through the struggle
'til we bring about some change
And we fight 'til we die
Or until we find our way

—*"Souls" Rob Murat*

Dedicated to Joshua and all of the visionaries and revolutionaries of tomorrow.

WALK WITH ME

"Walking down the streets of Woodland Avenue, standing at 58th Street and Chester Avenue, leaning in front of the store at 52nd and Baltimore are many with their backs against the wall, living black existential lives. Trying desperately not to go up north, making a way out of no way, moving through these streets in silence. Somewhere, there is a thug on Sigel Street in South Philly praying to God to spare his life."

—James G. Spady

"As I have walked among the desperate, rejected and angry young men, I have told them that Molotov cocktails and rifles would not solve their problems. . . . But they asked, and rightly so, 'What about Vietnam?' They asked if our nation wasn't using massive doses of violence to solve its problems, to bring about the changes it wanted. Their question hit home, and I knew that I could never again raise my voice against the violence of the oppressed in the ghettos without having first spoken clearly to the greatest purveyors of violence in the world today—my own country."

—Dr. Martin Luther King, Jr. "Beyond Vietnam"

"We at war. We at war with terrorism, racism but most of all, we at war with ourselves. . . . To the hustlers, killers, murderers, drug dealers . . . Jesus walks with them. To the victims of welfare . . . living in hell . . . Jesus walks with them."

—Kanye West "Jesus Walks"

Walk with me through the projects and tenement slums of America. 9/11 changed everything and nothing at all. Shocked and awed into a state of utter paralysis, America stands frozen at a historic crossroad between revolution and submission, overthrow and oppression, wealth and poverty, freedom and slavery, life and death. As American-made bombs fall on the innocent in Iraq and young Black children die in street violence in Washington, DC—the nation's capitol—where is God in this entire equation?

Having witnessed the horror of bodies floating through the feces-filled streets of New Orleans, one must ask: *Has God forsaken America?* As the public school system crumbles and prison cells overflow with the poor and uneducated, one wonders: *Is God blessing America or cursing it?* (Perhaps, more importantly, is America cursing itself?) Is God an active, living actor in this dangerous morality play? Or is America simply standing alone, cast adrift in a sea of perpetual wandering and war-mongering, slipping dangerously away from hurricane-ravaged shores of morality and decency with each exploding bomb, each collapsing tower, each burning mosque, each decaying corpse on the streets of New Orleans?

In the smoke and ashes of ground zero, both in New York and Fallujah, where is God? Does God walk with America? Does God walk with Iraq? As we comb through the ruins and wreckage of the democratic project in New Orleans, Baghdad, Beirut and elsewhere, the absence of divine, or even intelligent, guidance grows even more pronounced. (And the president and his generals are desperate for a victory of any kind, military or otherwise, as the specter of Vietnam settles hideously over the heads of George Bush, Dick Chaney, Condoleeza Rice and the bewildered military "planners" in the Pentagon.)

So is America starring alone in this epic, Hollywood-style contest of "good" and "evil," "hero" and "villain," "liberator" and "terrorist"? Is America fighting alone the "killers," the "thugs" and the "terrorists" in its midst? And who might these "killers," "thugs" and "terrorists" be? Who defines who is a "killer," a "thug," or a "terrorist" anyway? Who decides the punishment they should face either in this life or in the afterlife? And perhaps more immediately, who will determine the end of this "War on Terror" or even the longstanding "War on Drugs"? (The "War on Poverty" having long since been abandoned.) Did the so-called War on Terror begin on 9/12 or are the tangled roots of terror and terrorism planted deeply in the historical bedrock of America?

While President Bush reinstates previously discredited notions of the absolute power of governmental authority (sanctioned parsimoniously by various pastors and churches), it seems an appropriate time to call into question the validity of "God" in an age of war, terror and dread. In the words of writer James Baldwin, "If the concept of God has any validity or any use, it can only be to make us larger, freer and more loving. If God cannot do this, then it is time we got rid of Him." Judging by the current abysmal state of global affairs—the dire lack of freedom, justice and love in America and throughout the planet, "God" is a marked man. Indeed, as the cries of the oppressed in the Sudan, Lebanon, Palestine, South Central and elsewhere grow louder and stronger, God's validity, if not ongoing existence, is called into question.

In raising these troubling questions about the existence and allegiance of God, my primary concern is reminiscent of the theological concerns posed by the preeminent African American theologian Howard Thurman in his classic book *Jesus and the Disinherited*:

> "I can count on the fingers of one hand the number of times that I have heard a sermon on the meaning of religion, of Christianity, to the man who stands with his back against the wall. It is urgent that my meaning be crystal clear. The masses of men live with their backs against the wall. They are the poor, the disinherited, the dispossessed. What does our religion say to them?"

In this age of perpetual war, terror and dread, what is the religion of Jesus (or Muhammad, or Buddha, or Krishna, for that matter) to say to the poor, the outcasts, the oppressed and the have-nots in the barrios, ghettos and shantytowns of America, Nigeria, Israel, London, Liberia, Korea, Haiti, Jamaica, Sri Lanka, South Africa, Russia, Paris, Madrid, Brazil and other parts of the world? What is the religion of Jesus (and others) to say to those bloodied but unbowed Black, Latino and Native orphans of so-called American democracy—a grand experiment gone terribly wrong for so many? In fact, one wonders how this nation can even pretend to plant democracy in Iraq when democracy is dying on the vine in America.

If you doubt the failure of the democratic experiment in America, then walk with me while I introduce you to the have-nots and "thug niggas" of Philly, Miami, Detroit, Cleveland, Compton, Camden, Brooklyn, Baltimore, Chicago, Atlanta, St. Louis, Memphis, Houston, Little Rock, New Orleans,

East LA and an endless web of neglected communities of color that live under constant police assault and surveillance. Walk with me through the dark,
narrow corridors of Dade County jail where I counseled and prayed with my
young client, Darren, who faced first-degree murder charges and therefore,
the electric chair, if convicted.

As I visited Darren in a dark holding cell, his legs shackled like a rebellious
slave, I often wondered what hellish fate awaited not only him but many
Black men, women and children like him in this morally bankrupt society.
Sadly, during my years as a criminal defense attorney in Miami, Florida, I
witnessed first-hand Black and poor people being led disproportionately
down death row in a seriously flawed legal system. In a fit of anger, I asked
God the same unnerving existential questions that Tupac Shakur often wres-
tled with in his life and music: Is there hope for "ghetto" youth? Is there a
"ghetto" in Heaven? Is there Heaven for a "gangsta" or will God close the
gates? I wondered: Would these be Darren's last words? Were these the last
words of persecuted Black men such as Nat Turner, Gabriel Prosser, Medger
Evers, Malcolm X, MLK or even Jesus Christ as they faced death's gallows?
Yes, I said, even Jesus.

Hell, let's be clear on this. Jesus was a criminal. And he was Black. To
those in power, he was a bad ass "nigga." He had to be. Why else would the
authorities have crucified him? Did not Jesus defy the law? Did not he cohort
with prostitutes and drunkards—sinners all? Did not he roam from village to
village, ghetto to ghetto, inciting the masses and challenging the corrupt practices of the Pharisees and Sadducees—the high priests of his day? When Jesus chased the moneychangers out of the temple, angrily declaring that his father's house had been made "a den of robbers," he became a marked man. His
days were numbered. You always become a marked person when you mess
with folks' money. And Jesus messed with the chief priests' money. (Let's not
mention the shameful plight of our modern day Negro Pharisees and Sadducees—extraordinary moneychangers in their own right.)

Yes, Jesus was *publicly* indicted, convicted and executed for his crimes like
a common crook. It was as much of a spectacle as the hanging of Saddam
Hussein, that former American puppet, whose own trial was as suspect as a
poor Black man on trial in Texas. I suppose in a twisted sense, Saddam's
videotaped lynching was all part of that grand American tradition of "strange
fruit" hanging high and swinging low. And so when Black, Latino, Native
American and poor youth see precious dollars being flushed down the prover-
bial toilet in a failed war in Iraq, while victims of Hurricane Katrina and its
aftermath still don't have pots to piss in or windows to through it out of, then
Nina Simone's simmering racial indictment in *Mississippi Goddamn* boils
into a scathing rebuke of this entire God-forsaken nation: *America Goddamn!*

In the hearts and minds of disenfranchised and disaffected youth, *America Goddamn* becomes not only a prayer of damnation, but a rallying cry for insurrection. Rappers such as 'Lil Wayne, Rick Ross, NAS and others, who have spoken out against issues ranging from Hurricane Katrina to police brutality, are at the vanguard of an emerging global, Hip Hop-centered movement for economic freedom, social justice and divine retribution. One of the pioneers of this revolutionary movement, Tupac Shakur, speaks out of the mighty whirlwind of history: *"Ghetto born Black seeds still grow. We comin' back for everything you owe." America Goddamn.* This is the America, hell, the world, in which we have birthed this generation of youth. So why do many of us now turn away from them in fear, dread and loathing? Are these not our children? Are these not God's people?

If so, why do so many people, like comedian Bill Cosby, heartlessly condemn the poor and hungry for fighting (and at times, killing) to survive on cold city streets, while they turn a blind eye to the savage murder and plunder taking place in Baghdad, Beirut and Bethlehem? Wrong is wrong everywhere, whether in an alley in North Philly or in a bunker in Central Bagdad. Besides, haven't merciless American (read corporate) economic and foreign policies created the conditions for the "terror" raging on the nation's streets and throughout the world? As urban schools crumble and even menial jobs dry up for poor Black folks, why are so many shocked by the carnage in America's own backyard? Didn't Malcolm X warn that chickens one day come home to roost? Doesn't the Bible say that you reap what you sow? Forget the upper class rhetoric of Cosby who essentially blames the victims of poverty for their impoverished state. Listen to Tupac instead:

> "We're probably in hell already/Our dumb asses not knowin'/Everybody kissin' ass to go to Heaven ain't goin' . . . /The preacher want me buried/Why?/I know he a liar/Have you ever seen a crack-head/That's eternal fire . . . /Givin' up cash to the leaders/Knowin' damn well they ain't gonna feed us . . . /They say Jesus is a kind man/Well, he should understand times in this crime land. . ."[1]

Surely, Jesus understands. Jesus spent much of his ministry helping thieves, whores, lepers and sinners. The life of Jesus is the story of truth being spoken to power. In the end, it is the story of that truth being crushed by power but ultimately rising again. It is also the story of an individual and a race of people navigating the explosive minefields of race, religion and class. This is a story I understand all too well.

Born and raised in a working-class, Catholic family in Philadelphia, I grew up at a time in America, not unlike today, when justice and equality, especially for Black and poor people, seemed elusive if not outright illusive. This was the late 1960s and early 1970s. This was the Philadelphia of MOVE, Frank L. Rizzo, the

Black Panther Party, Cecil B. Moore, the Nation of Islam and Mumia Abu Ja-
mal, who is currently "sitting" on death row. (Sitting on death row is presumably
a more desirable position than walking down death row, although I'm not quite
sure that there is much difference, existentially speaking.)

As a young child, I witnessed brutal police beatings and bombings of those
apparently presumed guilty. This was my first taste of terror—State terror—
decades before 9/11. Terror leaves a bitter taste in your mouth. Black folks
and poor folks have never been strangers to terror and terrorism. My parents
were so poor that they attended a special school in Philadelphia for malnourished children. My parents learned in childhood the true meaning of terror.
Poverty is terror. Hunger is terror. Police brutality is terror. Sleeping under a
bridge or in an old, broken-down Chevy is terror. Bin Laden didn't tell Black
and poor folks anything we didn't already know about terror—terror is intentional, calculated and designed to destroy as many as possible. By the grace
of God, I am a survivor of terror—not Islamic terror, but American terror.

Growing up in the streets of West Philadelphia, I witnessed raw terror—
insane acts of police brutality and gang violence. Black on Black violence was
incited in order to keep the community divided and hence, weak and power-
less. (Ultimately, it failed on all counts as the community found tremendous
strength and power in unity.) The long arm of the law was used to keep the
Black "natives" from crossing into the territory of the white "pioneers" who
had settled a "colony" euphemistically known as the University of Pennsylvania. As a child, my friends and I often rode our bikes on campus, racing play-
fully down the walkways as students and campus police cursed our presence,
if not our very existence. At such a young and precocious age, I swore that one
day I would attend and graduate from the university as an act of resistance and
revenge. When I graduated from there in June of 1988, I had achieved a victory not only for myself but for my family and community as well.

Interestingly, my Ivy League education paled in comparison to the life lessons of integrity, ingenuity, loyalty and morality that I learned while running
the streets of West Philly. The players, pimps, prostitutes, addicts, hustlers
and gang-bangers taught me more about life, the law and God than any soci-
ology course at PENN, any criminal justice course at Georgetown Law
School, and any theology course at Harvard Divinity School. The so-called
ghetto was the perfect classroom in which to learn how to survive and thrive
in America. Though it was challenging at times, I grew up in a vibrant, dynamic neighborhood, filled with honorable and decent folks. This is not to either romanticize or demonize my neighborhood, which was widely known as
the Black Bottom. My neighborhood certainly wasn't the setting for the
Cosby Show. Thankfully, it also wasn't the setting for New Jack City. Instead,
it was a place, perhaps not unlike Jerusalem in the time of Jesus, where the
good, the bad and the ugly had much to teach and learn.

Having grown up in Philly at that particular time, I would later understand intuitively the challenges faced by many of my clients in Miami, particularly young Black men such as Darren. Having witnessed it first hand, I knew the bottomless depth of police violence and oppression in poor communities. I knew all too well the death and destruction created in the 1990s by outside forces flooding the so-called ghetto with crack cocaine and guns. I also knew the unholy pain and suffering of poverty caused by structural unemployment. So in the darkness of Darren's jail cell and in the shadows of Tupac's grave, I prayed to God for answers to the conditions facing many Black youth. In the silence of my grief over the predicament of my people, I began to listen even more closely and less judgmentally to rap music. In so doing, I identified the existence of a powerful theology shared by many rap artists, particularly those self-identified as thugs and gangsters.

In 1996, as a result of deep reflection on Hip Hop culture and consciousness, I coined the term Thugology—thug theology—as an accurate description of the profound theological reflections of rap artists such as Tupac, the Outlawz, Jay Z, NAS, Mac Mall, DMX, Biggie Smalls, Beanie Sigel, Scarface, Trick Daddy and others whose music critically challenges mainstream interpretations of God and religion. In addition, Thugology, acknowledges the lived experiences of all seemingly outcast groups such as "thugs," Blacks, Latinos, Native Americans, and the poor. From a theological perspective, Thugology underscores the role of salvation and liberation played by Jesus, a criminal himself, who promised Paradise to the repentant criminal crucified beside him. Lyrically, NAS captures precisely the biblical and theological essence of Thugology when he boldly proclaims: "God love us hood niggas/Cuz next to Jesus on the cross wuz the crook niggas/But he forgive us."

Taking God's mercy and grace to another level, Tupac reflects: "I believe God blesses those who hustle." This is true. I am a living witness. There is hope in the valley. In this age of war, terror and dread, Thugology is *the* balm in Gilead to "thugs," "have-nots" and "outcasts" who pray to God while struggling to survive on mean city streets. These praying "niggas" are the pre-9/11 survivors. They don't live at ground zero. They live below it. In the words of Beanie Sigel: "We grind from the bottom just to make it to the bottom."

9/11 changed everything and nothing at all. America Goddamn.

NOTE

1. Shakur, Tupac "Blasphemy" Featured on the Album *The Don Killuminati: The 7 Day Theory* (Death Row/Interscope Records 1996).

Chapter Six

Strategies for Raising Poverty in America as a Violation of International Human Rights Law

Beth Lyon

Now a days things ain't ok.
I guess that you could say that life ain't easy
We wish and pray for better days to come
But every single day seems like yesterday

— *"Souls" Rob Murat*

"As we move to make justice a reality on the international scale, as we move to make justice a reality in this nation, how will the struggle be waged?"

—Martin Luther King

The United States' famously prosperous middle class overshadows the developing world that lies within its borders. The divide between America's rich and poor is striking: Data from the Congressional Budget Office indicates that the gap between the United States' rich and poor has more than doubled in the last 30 years. In contrast to most other industrialized countries, the United States has no federal constitutional and scant state constitutional protections for substantive economic and social rights, such as the right to housing or adequate nutrition. In 1996, the Personal Responsibility and Work Opportunity Reconciliation Act of 1996 (PRWORA) dismantled the national welfare entitlement, significantly decreased federal spending for welfare, and devolved control over much of the federal spending to the states for state-level management of the social safety net. This shift accompanied widespread privatization of the welfare delivery system. PRWORA pushed thousands of people off the welfare rolls and sent them deeper into poverty. According the 2004 U.S. Census Bureau's Report, the poverty rate rose from 12.1 percent in 2002 to 12.5 percent in 2003. In only one year, 1.3 million additional Americans found themselves living in poverty, bringing the nation's total number of impoverished citizens to 35.9 million people. The 2006 UNDP Human Development Report ranks the wealthiest 20 percent of Americans at the top of its list, while the poorest 20 percent of Americans find themselves ranked below the Human Development Index for Argentina and equal to that of Cuba. Still, even with the white American upper and middle classes factored in, giving the United States the third highest per capita income in the world, this country has the third highest poverty rate in the industrialized world and falls behind most other industrialized nations in life expectancy and functional literacy.

After decades of political isolation, concerns about social justice and poverty alleviation have reached the mainstream international human rights and development agendas. The shift in emphasis carries with it increased international resources for addressing human deprivation. International institutions have much to offer advocates for the poor in the United States.

Beset by U.S. welfare reform, which many critics characterize as "a war on the poor," and silenced by the cutoff of funds to legal aid organizations, poor people in the United States have begun looking to international institutions for support. A coalition of domestic and international advocates filed an unprecedented complaint about U.S. economic and social rights violations that is pending with the Inter-American Commission on Human Rights. Over the last 20 years, a handful of international economic rights non-governmental organizations (NGOs) have begun U.S.-focused programs, while increasing numbers of domestic anti-poverty groups are reaching out for international standards and resources to protect their constituencies.

This chapter provides an overview of the international economic and social rights law sources available to U.S. anti-poverty advocates, strategies for seeking the intervention of international institutions, and domestic strategies for directly confronting U.S. adjudicators and policymakers with their obligations under international economic, social, and cultural rights law.

INTERNATIONAL ECONOMIC, SOCIAL, AND CULTURAL RIGHTS SOURCES FOR U.S. ADVOCATES

As the United States allows its poor people to sink deeper into hunger and deprivation, the international human rights community is devoting increased resources to promoting and protecting economic, social, and cultural rights, resulting in a rich body of substantive standards and protections. The unique matrix of protections binding on the United States arises from this country's selective and somewhat schizophrenic ratification of international human rights treaties.

The 1948 Universal Declaration of Human Rights (UDHR or Universal Declaration), shaped and supported by U.S. officials, enumerates a near full range of economic, social, and cultural rights, in addition to civil and political rights. The UDHR's framers intended for one formal human rights treaty to follow, codifying the UDHR, but Cold War politics intervened and the United States insisted on partitioning economic, social, and cultural rights, which it considered communist, from civil and political rights, which it considered Western.

The result was two international treaties: the International Covenant on Civil and Political Rights (ICCPR or Civil and Political Rights Covenant), and the International Covenant on Economic, Social and Cultural Rights (ICESCR or ESC Rights Covenant). The ICESCR binds its signatories to "take steps, individually and through international assistance and co-operation . . . to the maximum of its available resources, with a view to achieving progressively the full realization of [economic, social and cultural] rights by all appropriate means, including particularly the adoption of legislative measures." The concept of progressive achievement does not figure in the UN's Civil and Political Rights Covenant, leading the U.S. government to argue that civil and political rights are intended to be immediately implemented by courts, but that economic, social and cultural rights can only be realized over the long term and thus are not suitable for adjudication by courts.

Throughout the Cold War, the United States routinely took the position that economic, social, and cultural rights were not justifiable and should not be considered rights. There have been a few exceptions to this stance: 1) President Carter's 1977 pre-ratification signature of the UN's ESC Rights Covenant and 2) the U.S. participation in the Conference on Security and Co-operation in Europe Final Act, which included economic and social rights language. In 1999, U.S. officials made a few lower-profile statements at the United Nations recognizing the indivisibility and interdependence of all human rights, representing a temporary reversal of position during the Clinton administration. However, today the U.S. position remains opposed to economic, social and cultural rights. The 1996 World Food Summit, at which the United States angered the international community with its insistence that there is no right to food, is a good example of the U.S. government's increasingly contrarian view. Despite President Carter's initial signature on the UN ESC Rights Covenant, the United States has never ratified the treaty, and the United States has also declined to ratify both the American Convention on Human Rights and the Additional Protocol to the American Convention on Human Rights in the Area of Economic, Social and Cultural Rights.

Meanwhile, however, the United States *has* opened limited avenues for advocacy on social and economic rights. Although the UN's Civil and Political

Rights Covenant (ICCPR) does not contain the full range of ESC rights available through its twin covenant, it does offer some opportunities to U.S. anti-poverty advocates. Apart from recognizing the importance of economic, social, and cultural rights as a general matter, the ICCPR explicitly protects many rights with a direct bearing on economic justice, including the right to life, protection of the family and child, freedom from forced labor, and non-discrimination. The ICCPR also protects cultural rights, such as the right to use a minority language or religion. The United States has ratified two additional major UN treaties that protect specific vulnerable groups and include economic, social, and cultural rights, as well as the civil and political rights: the Protocol Relating to the Status of Refugees, and the International Convention on the Elimination of All Forms of Racial Discrimination (Race Discrimination Convention). On a parallel track, the United States partially participated in adopting Inter-American regional human rights law, by supporting the American Declaration on the Rights and Duties of Man (American Declaration). Finally, the North American Free Trade Agreement (NAFTA) treaty concluded between the United States, Mexico, and Canada carried with it two side agreements designed to protect labor and environmental rights in the signatory countries.

MATRIX OF PROTECTIONS

Thus, from the point of view of U.S. anti-poverty advocates, the primary legal sources for international economic, social, and cultural rights are the Universal Declaration, the UN's ESC Rights Covenant (by virtue of the U.S. signature), the UN's Civil and Political Rights Covenant, the Refugee Protocol, the UN's Race Discrimination Convention, and the American Declaration, each of which binds the United States to a greater or lesser extent. The side agreements to the NAFTA also are important international sources committing the United States to uphold its own labor and environmental protection laws. Another potential but untested source of international economic and social rights standards is customary law.

INTERNATIONAL STRATEGIES FOR
U.S. ANTI-POVERTY ADVOCATES

Bringing domestic policy into conformity with international law involves both exposing factual situations to the international institutions and importing standards directly into domestic advocacy. Many human rights mechanisms and institutions may be or have proven useful to the U.S. fight against domestic poverty. These include both treaty bodies charged with overseeing implementation of the human rights treaties described above and other entities that are less formal or permanent.

UN HUMAN RIGHTS COMMITTEE

The UN Human Rights Committee is charged with monitoring adherence to the UN's Civil and Political Rights Covenant, or ICCPR. The United States ratified the ICCPR in 1992, but declared it "non-self-executing," or unenforceable in a court of law in the absence of implementing legislation. Implementing legislation has not been forthcoming, nor has the United States ratified the protocol to the ICCPR giving the Human Rights Committee jurisdiction over individual complaints about ICCPR violations.

The Committee does, however, hold public hearings on each state party's compliance with the Covenant. In the United States' first two hearings before the Committee, held in 1995 and 2006, U.S. NGOs strongly influenced the questions Committee members posed to the U.S. governmental representatives. The Committee also accepted reports and heard testimony directly from American NGOs.

In its concluding observations to the United States initial compliance report, the Committee expressed concern at "the high incidence of poverty, sickness and alcoholism among Native Americans . . . [and the fact that] disproportionate numbers of Native Americans, African Americans, Hispanics and single parent families headed by women live below the poverty line and that one in four children under six live in poverty." The Committee also "note[d] with concern . . . that poverty and lack of access to education adversely affect persons belonging to these groups in their ability to enjoy rights under the Covenant on the basis of equality." In its most recent report on the United States, issued in 2006, the Committee made two important statements with regard to poverty: "The Committee is concerned with reports that some 50% of homeless people are African American although they constitute only 12% of the United States population." The Committee also recommended that "in the aftermath of Hurricane Katrina, the State party should increase its efforts to ensure that the rights of the poor, and in particular African-Americans, are fully taken into consideration in the reconstruction plans with regard to access to housing, education and healthcare."

The United States' next report to the Human Rights Committee is due August 1, 2010, and anti-poverty advocates in America can participate in the process by filing parallel reports commenting on social justice. The previous statements of the committee indicate that it is particularly amenable to criticizing the United States on poverty issues that have a disproportionate race or gender impact.

COMMITTEE ON THE ELIMINATION
OF RACIAL DISCRIMINATION

The Committee on the Elimination of Racial Discrimination monitors compliance with the CERD. The United States ratified the CERD in 1994, but declared the treaty "non-self-executing." The treaty contains many provisions supportive of economic and social rights. In particular, Article 5 requires that states parties "eliminate" racial discrimination, and "guarantee the right of everyone, without distinction as to race, color, or national or ethnic origin, to equality before the law." The CERD notes everyone's right to enjoy economic, social, and cultural rights, particularly: "[t]he rights to work, to free choice of employment, to just and favorable conditions of work, to protection against unemployment, to equal pay for equal work, to just and favorable remuneration; . . . to form and join trade unions; . . . [t]he right to housing; . . . [t]he right to public health, medical care, social security and social services; . . . [t]he right to education and training; . . . [and] [t]he right to equal participation in cultural activities."

CERD Article 2(2) also imposes upon states parties the affirmative duty to take "special and concrete measures to ensure the adequate development and protection of certain racial groups or individuals belonging to them, for the purpose of guaranteeing them the full and equal enjoyment of human rights and fundamental freedoms." In contrast to U.S. equal protection jurisprudence, this language suggests that a disparate impact analysis, demonstrating relative disadvantage of a protected class, with or without a showing of discriminatory governmental motive, is sufficient to trigger the duty to take affirmative action. This interpretation is supported by the treaty's definition of "racial discrimination" as any distinction that has the "purpose or effect" of impairing essential human rights.

The CERD requires states parties to submit biennial reports on compliance with the treaty for consideration and comment. In addition, under Article 11 of the CERD, the Committee on the Elimination of Racial Discrimination is empowered to consider statements from other states party to the CERD alleging that the United States "is not giving effect to the provisions of this Convention." As with the UN Human Rights Committee and the ICCPR, the United States has not recognized the CERD Committee's competence to hear individual complaints against it, so for the present time, U.S. NGOs must focus on influencing the Committee through the reporting process or the Article 11 state-to-state process. A joint NGO parallel report on U.S. compliance with CERD, released by the World Organization Against Torture in anticipation of the first U.S. report, argued that through recent developments ending affirmative action in higher education programs, the United States has violated its Article 2 obligation to ensure the adequate development of racial minorities. Groups like the World Organization that have experience dealing with international monitoring bodies are typically open to collaboration with domestic NGOs and advocates.

In response to the first U.S. reports, in 2001 the Committee on the Elimination of Race Discrimination rebuked the United States on the racial impact of poverty in America. The Committee observed that "[W]hile noting the numerous laws, institutions and measures designed to eradicate racial discrimination affecting the equal enjoyment of economic, social and cultural rights, the Committee is concerned about persistent disparities in the enjoyment of, in particular, the right to adequate housing, equal opportunities for education and employment and access to public and private health care. The Committee recommends the State party to take all appropriate measures, including special measures according to article 2, paragraph 2 of the Convention, to ensure the right of everyone, without discrimination as to race, color, or national or ethnic origin to the enjoyment of [economic and social] rights. . ."

The Committee went on to state that "[w]ith regard to affirmative action, the Committee notes with concern the position taken by the State party that the provisions of the Convention permit, but do not require States parties to adopt affirmative action measures to ensure the adequate development and protection of certain racial, ethnic or national groups. The Committee emphasizes that the adoption of special measures by States parties, when the circumstances so warrant, such as in the case of persistent disparities, is an obligation stemming from article 2, paragraph 2 of the Convention." These statements demonstrate that the Committee on Racial Discrimination, like the Human Rights Committee, is likely to be most open to concerns about social justice in America framed as discrimination arguments.

UN COMMITTEE ON ECONOMIC, SOCIAL AND CULTURAL RIGHTS

A 1985 UN Economic and Social Council resolution created the Committee on Economic, Social and Cultural Rights, to monitor compliance with the ICESCR. Although the United States' failure to ratify the ICESCR means that the Committee is not yet seized with monitoring economic, social, and cultural rights in the United States, the Committee has directed some informal efforts at U.S. ratification. The Committee's activist stance on economic, social, and cultural rights, and a thoughtful body of comments and reports, make its interpretations authoritative. The materials are an important resource for any anti-poverty advocate. In the author's view, what makes the Committee unique is that the three main goals of the Committee's work are to move governments to: 1) acknowledge and measure poverty in a way that identifies its effect on the most vulnerable members of society; 2) develop and implement concrete plans aiming at measurable goals for bettering the condition of the most economically disadvantaged members of society; and 3) continually work to lessen the economic consequences of discrimination.

SOUTH AFRICAN CONSTITUTIONAL COURT

South Africa is making a concerted effort to give its new constitution's economic and social rights real meaning in a very difficult fiscal and political context. Several landmark cases from the South African Constitutional Court, thoroughly documented in U.S. commentary, also offer important guidance and inspiration for U.S. social justice movements.

INTER-AMERICAN COMMISSION ON HUMAN RIGHTS

The Inter-American Commission on Human Rights is the human rights adjudicator of first instance in the Organization of American States (OAS). Because the United States supported the American Declaration but has not ratified the American Convention on Human Rights, only the Inter-American Commission, as opposed to the Inter-American Court on Human Rights, is empowered to hear cases against the United States, and in so doing it may only apply the Declaration. As noted above, the United States also has not ratified the Additional Protocol to the American Convention on Human Rights in the Area of Economic, Social and Cultural Rights, which entered into force in 1999. However, the Commission has issued many innovative rulings on civil and political rights matters in favor of individual U.S. petitioners.

The Inter-American Commission on Human Rights is beginning to spend more time on economic, social, and cultural rights, and has held hearings on such issues as the right to education and the rights of migrant workers in the hemisphere. In addition, the Poor People's Economic Human Rights Campaign complaint to the Commission mentioned above signals an important challenge to the 1996 welfare reform, and is expected to provide a forum for airing conditions of poverty throughout the country. Moreover, over the past decade the Commission has been investigating the condition of migrant workers in the United States through its Special Rapporteur on Migrant Workers and their Families, and a group of unauthorized immigrant workers filed a petition against the United States with the Commission in 2006.

COMMISSION FOR LABOR COOPERATION AND THE COMMISSION FOR ENVIRONMENTAL COOPERATION

The NAFTA treaty took effect in 1994. For the first time in the history of free trade zones, the states negotiated inter-governmental mechanisms for adjudicating labor and environmental rights complaints in conjunction with a trade-liberalizing treaty. The new NAFTA procedures provide an additional avenue for U.S. advocates.

The two NAFTA side agreements, the North American Agreement on Labor Cooperation and the North American Agreement on Environmental Cooperation respectively created the Commission for Labor Cooperation and the Commission for Environmental Cooperation. The commissions hear complaints from non-governmental entities alleging that member countries are failing to enforce their own labor and environmental standards. The gap between standards and enforcement leaves fertile ground for action, but like most international rights bodies, the commissions are limited by insufficient funding and enforcement powers. Extraordinary violations can result in a recommendation of trade sanctions, although the most likely result of a successful complaint is a "consultation" by the relevant agencies of the three governments on the problem the petitioner identified.

As of March 2004, the Commission for Labor Cooperation had received nine complaints against the United States. While one complaint was not accepted for review, the other eight have had some social justice impact in the United States. Outcomes have included ministerial consultations leading to Joint Declarations among Canada, Mexico, and the United States; the issuance of a Memorandum of Understanding between the U.S. Immigration and Naturalization Services and the U.S. Department of Labor concerning wage and hour complaints of immigrant workers; and commitments to more widely disseminate bilingual government notification of rights to migrant workers. A complaint filed in early 2006 asserted the rights of immigrant workers to legal representation.

EXTRA-CONVENTIONAL MECHANISMS FOR BRINGING INTERNATIONAL ECONOMIC, SOCIAL, AND CULTURAL RIGHTS TO THE UNITED STATES

The United Nations and OAS human rights regimes abound with non-adjudicatory human rights activities. Special Rapporteurs and working groups focused on different aspects of poverty and vulnerable groups conduct missions and release reports that can be helpful to domestic litigation and policy work. The proceedings and final conclusions of UN conferences, such as the 1994 International Conference on Population and Development in Cairo, which focused on women's reproductive health, and the 1996 UN

Conference on Human Settlements (Habitat II), can be important for exposing poverty in the United States.

In October 1994, Maurice Glélé-Ahanhanzo, the UN Special Rapporteur of the Commission on Human Rights on contemporary forms of racism, racial discrimination, xenophobia and related intolerance, conducted a mission to the United States. In his 1995 report, the Special Rapporteur carefully documented statistics reflecting the drastically poorer health, education, housing, and employment conditions racial minorities experience in the United States. The report was infused with economic and social rights concepts, even ascribing the United States' contemporaneous ratifications of the ICCPR and the CERD to an "emphasis . . . on the unity of the rights of the human person, namely, the interdependence and indivisibility of civil and political rights and economic, social and cultural rights."

U.S. advocates frequently communicate with extra-conventional international mechanisms. In fall 2006, for example, the UN General Assembly convened a plenary meeting it called a "high level dialogue" to discuss the situation of migrants. Many U.S. NGOs, including immigrants' rights groups, church organizations, and unions, submitted reports and delivered remarks at both the preparatory meetings and before the assembled delegations.

INTERNATIONAL LABOUR ORGANIZATION

Probably the oldest intergovernmental human rights organization, the International Labour Organization (ILO) is responsible for monitoring a series of wide-ranging labor protection conventions. Complaint and report review procedures are available; however, the United States ratified just a handful of the most technical conventions, including only two of what the ILO defines as its eight "fundamental" conventions (the Abolition of Forced Labour Convention and the Elimination of the Worst Forms of Child Labour Convention) and one of the four "priority" conventions (the Convention on Tripartite Consultation). The ILO Committee on Freedom of Association asserts jurisdiction over the United States by virtue of the United States' membership in the UN. For example, the Committee recently ruled against the United States in a complaint lodged by the AFL-CIO and the Federation of Mexican Workers, ruling that the United States should reverse its practice of excluding unauthorized immigrant workers from full protection under the National Labor Relations Act remedies scheme.

DOMESTIC STRATEGIES

Ultimately, the reason why advocates should access the international mechanisms described above is to elicit international suasion to convince domestic decision-makers to comply with international standards. Thus it is important to confront domestic decision-makers with international standards directly. Civil rights advocates are well in advance of the social justice community in using international norms to influence domestic policy and litigation. Some of the many opportunities for domestic enforcement activities include educating the public, presenting international standards in domestic litigation, and campaigning for treaty ratification.

PUBLIC EDUCATION

The U.S. legal framework is strongly rights-oriented, but almost exclusively in the field of civil and political rights. Most explanations of this country's anti-economic rights culture point to our eighteenth century constitution, now said to be the oldest constitution in the world. In American political history, the two significant expansions of resource allocation for anti-poverty measures followed dramatic national events creating a collective shift in political will: the Great Depression, which led to the New Deal, and the assassination of John F. Kennedy, which led to the War on Poverty. Several groups, including the National Center for Human Rights Education in Atlanta, are attempting to inculcate an economic rights culture by conducting grassroots outreach rooted in international rights. Food First, based in Oakland, California, and the Washington, D.C.-based Institute for Policy Studies ran a series of "Economic Rights Bus Tours" to impoverished areas. The Kensington Welfare Rights Union of Philadelphia also organizes marches and bus tours, and several of their marches ended at the steps of intergovernmental institutions.

INVOKING INTERNATIONAL STANDARDS
IN DOMESTIC LITIGATION

Although PRWORA extinguished the general welfare entitlement, many aspects of welfare policy find review in litigation, most commonly decisions to terminate benefits. Policy challenges to the PRWORA also have been successful, most notably in the 1999 U.S. Supreme Court case *Saenz v. Roe*, in which the Court struck down PWRORA-sanctioned differentiation between long-term and short-term residents for the purposes of welfare benefits. It appears, however, that economic justice advocates have not made systematic attempts to bring international economic, social, and cultural rights to the attention of the U.S. judicial branch. Interestingly enough, at least nine reported U.S. court cases cite to the ICESCR. However, the United States failure to ratify the ICESCR or to pass implementing legislation importing the CERD into domestic statutory law means that a U.S. court is unlikely to rely heavily on international standards as binding law on poverty-related issues.

International customary law is a recognized source of U.S. federal law. Customary law is a rule that is widely documented and followed, through the general assent of states, and has been at least tacitly accepted by the United States in its custom and practice. Once recognized as customary law, an international norm is binding on the United States even in the absence of a treaty or domestic obligation on point. In the landmark case of *Filartiga v. Peña-Irala*, decided in 1980, the federal Second Circuit recognized and applied an international customary norm prohibiting torture. The United States' persistent public refusals to recognize economic, social, and cultural rights have heretofore all but blocked a customary law analysis. The U.S. governments' recent statements at the United Nations recognizing the validity of economic, social, and cultural rights may signal an opportunity to argue for a customary norm of the most egregious economic rights violations, like states' refusals to provide for malnourished and homeless children.

In addition to making international law arguments directly in complaints, U.S. courts can be educated about new international human rights standards through *amicus curiae* (friend of the court) briefs, judicial training, and bar activities. These promotional methods have been used successfully by proponents of international standards in the U.S. refugee protection regime. For example, in *INS v. Cardoza-Fonseca*, decided in 1987, the U.S. Supreme Court found for the asylum-seeker and noted that, because Congress had written the asylum laws with an intent to conform U.S. law to an international refugee treaty, the Supreme Court was "guided" by the UN High Commissioner for Refugees' handbook on determining refugee status. The Supreme Court further noted that the handbook "has been widely considered useful in giving content to the obligations that the Protocol establishes." The pro-individual-rights outcome and encouraging language were the results of long efforts by domestic and international refugee lawyers.

Three recent decisions by the U.S. Supreme Court also referred to international and foreign law as supportive or even persuasive in the course of making important civil rights advances: the abolition of the death penalty for juvenile offenders and mentally retarded prisoners, and the abolition of anti-sodomy statutes. Advocates for the poor in the United States should find ways to make relevant international standards similarly useful to U.S. adjudicators.

ACCESSION CAMPAIGNS

Activists can also work for U.S. accession to treaties that can then be invoked directly on behalf of poor people in U.S. litigation. Ratification of a treaty requires the "advice and consent" of the Senate through a 2/3 majority vote. Because of longstanding opposition in the U.S. Senate and early failures of leadership by the U.S. bar, United States' ratification of human rights treaties lags behind most other countries in the world. Many un-ratified human rights treaties have a direct bearing on economic justice, namely the ICESCR (ratified as of December 2006 by 155 countries, and signed by the U.S. in 1977 but never ratified), the first Optional Protocol to the International Covenant on Civil and Political Rights (ratified, as of December 2006, by 109 countries), the Convention on the Elimination of All Forms of Discrimination against Women (ratified, as of December 2006, by 185 countries, and signed by the U.S. in 1980 but never ratified), the Convention on the Rights of the Child (ratified, as of December 2006, by 193 countries, and signed by the U.S. in 1995 but never ratified), the International Convention on the Protection of the Rights of All Migrant Workers and Members of Their Families (ratified, as of December 2006, by 34 countries), the American Convention on Human Rights, the Additional Protocol to the American Convention on Human Rights in the Area of Economic, Social and Cultural Rights, and most of the ILO conventions. Moreover, the United States should be lobbied to make a declaration under Article 14 of the CERD, which will enable U.S. residents to make individual petitions to the Committee on the Elimination of Racial Discrimination.

With the exception of an Amnesty International-led campaign focused on the Convention on the Elimination of All Forms of Discrimination Against Women, few active ratification efforts are currently underway. Municipal "ratifications," or endorsements, of the ICESCR and other international standards have taken place around the country, which may help lay the foundation of public opinion for the day when Senate action seems possible.

CONCLUSION

The United States' pre-economic-rights legal culture and low per capita spending on poverty alleviation has resulted in what Food First calls "the new American crisis . . . of barely-hidden, widespread desperation and structural poverty." As U.S. poverty deepens, international economic and social rights standards have begun to filter into the United States. Domestic and international advocacy groups have begun to interact with one another, and with the international institutions devoted to economic and social rights and human-focused development. Many opportunities exist to strengthen these ties and to bring international human rights standards to bear for poor people in the United States.

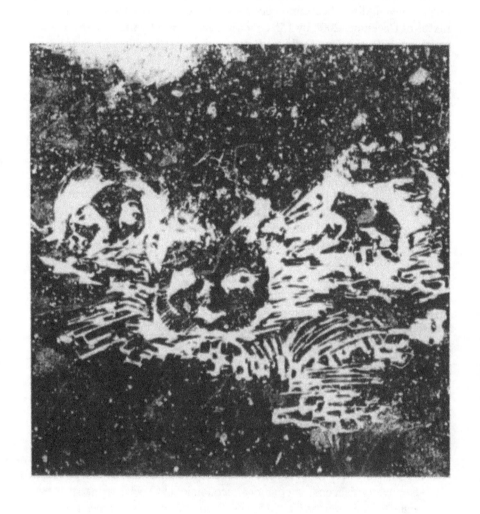

Chapter Seven

Silent Pulpits: A Historical Examination of Black Christian Engagement with Capitalism

Charles Lattimore Howard

There's something 'bout the souls
Of my people
I'm talking bout the souls
Of my beautiful folks
And even through we poor
We hopeful
Even though we poor
Oh We hope

—*"Souls" Rob Murat*

"Why are there no genuinely radical and independent voices coming from our leaders today? Why do they pose alternatives that exist only within capitalism, a system which offers no hope for the masses of blacks? Personally I like Andy Young, NAACP, Urban League, Jesse Jackson and our Black elected officials, and I do not wish to minimize the hard work and devotion they have given on our behalf. The same is true for our ministers and theologians of the gospel. But what I find missing in what they propose are genuinely new visions of the social order. Perhaps what we need today is to return to that "good old time religion" of our grandparents and combine with it a Marxist critique of society. Together Black religion and Marxist philosophy may show us the way to build a completely new society. With that combination, we may be able to realize in the society the freedom of which we sing and pray for in the Black church."[1]

—James Cone "The Black Church and Marxism:
What do they have to say to each other?"

Ministers and theologians, both ordained and lay, of the African Diaspora, have always served as leaders in the international struggle for liberation and the bettering of our society. God has spoken and continues to speak through that diverse segment of the Body of Christ which has come to be known as the Black Church. From the movements to abolish slavery here in the United States to the Civil Rights Movement, The Black Church has "spoken truth to power" and worked to revolutionize our young nation and ultimately the entire world. Are there still voices from within the Black Church questioning not only the suffering of its people, but the systemic issues that may be causing that suffering? In particular, are there voices questioning the suffering caused by poverty and the systemic forces/issues that are causing that poverty?

It is the purpose of this brief essay to consider these questions. Here we will first consider the ways in which capitalism, particularly the neoliberal globalized form of capitalism, and several other systemic challenges are destroying the majority of the people in this world (and most of them are people of color). Next a history of Black and Black Christian socialists will be explored as they have offered reformative and revolutionary alternatives to capitalism. Next some ways to challenge ministers and congregations to seek alternatives to capitalism will be put forth. Finally some powerful yet dangerous alternatives already in practice (or already proposed) will be shared. This call and the combination of Black, Christian, and Socialist, are especially dangerous at a time when triumphant capitalism reigns, the prosperity gospel is the dominant word preached, and sisters and brothers of the African Diaspora still face oppression on a daily basis. It should be stated outright that poverty is not the result of solely capitalism, but this essay, while referencing the other causes and sustainers of poverty, will be primarily focusing on capitalism.

For nearly four hundred years[2] women and men of African decent (or ascent) have struggled against, and by God's grace overcome various forms of oppression in this land and nation. During their earliest centuries in what became the United States of America, the major struggle was for the abolition of the gruesome dehumanizing practice of human chattel slavery. After the legislative and actual end to slavery the struggle moved to the acquisition and securing of different civil rights that according to The Constitution, are guaranteed to all citizens of the United States of America. Within the fights against slavery and for civil rights, a number of other battles were and continue to be fought such as gender rights for Black women, equal treatment in the judicial system, appropriate inclusion in all aspects of society and so much more. And while it may not be as visible today as it was in the 1960's, the struggle continues.

Today the great principality that we are wrestling with is not as obviously oppressive. The current Goliath that we are (or in many cases are not) engaging with is not nearly as blatantly cruel and deadly. Today, African Americans and the rest of the world find ourselves coexisting during a period of neo-liberal globalization that is spreading the suffocating smoke cloud of capitalism, which, among several factors, is a major cause of poverty in America and in the world.

This is not news. This is a conversation (critiques of various forms of capitalism) that has been occurring in various forms over the last few centuries. When alternatives to capitalism are presented within Christian and wider circles, the response is often a referral to Niebuhrian Christian realism. And as the idealism (utopianism?) of the Social Gospelers and their socialism gave way to Christian realism, the realism too gave way to liberation theologies.[3] Today, our project, the project of this text, is to demonstrate that it is possible to critique capitalism and the resulting poverty whether you prescribe to democratic or any other type of socialism, or not. In fact this critique and intentional action is necessary.

It is important here to define both neoliberal globalization and capitalism as well as to describe what I mean by poverty. It should be said outright that there are varying definitions and perspectives on these three major realities within our society.[4] The following definitions will be primarily from the AGAPE Background Document put forth by the World Council of Churches for the first two and from Dr. Mark Rank's book *One Nation, Underprivileged* and from Dr. Michael Katz's *The Undeserving Poor* for the latter.

After the World Council of Churches gathering at Harrare, Zimbabwe (1998), a committee was formed to explore "the question of how churches and the wider ecumenical family can respond to the human tragedies rooted in the project of economic globalization.[5]" Here they make an important distinction between economic globalization and the other types of globalization that may not be as exploitative in nature (though these other modes of globalization are often exploited for economic growth). Development and technology in the fields of transportation and communication for example, have contributed to the globalizing process that our world is presently engaged in.

In his *Atlantic* article "Jihad vs. McWorld" Benjamin R. Barber defines globalization, which he calls the dynamic of McWorld, as follows:

"Four imperatives make up the dynamic of McWorld: A market imperative (common market with common language, common currency producing common behaviors) a resource imperative (after the depletion of resources, the wealthiest nations end up dependent on the resources of other nations while many others are left in desperate straits.), an information-technology imperative (the border-crossing ability of modes of transportation, hardware, software, and cultural production without being particularly democratic), and an ecological imperative (not only the draining of resources for a world size demand, but the hindering of modernization in some areas that we "need to remain green." By shrinking the world and diminishing the salience of national borders, these imperatives have in combination achieved a considerable victory over factiousness and particularism, and not least of all over their most virulent traditional form—nationalism."[6]

This committee of the WCC was charged with the task of envisioning and articulating how Christians might live out their faiths in the context of economic globalization. They were to present their findings before the WCC gathering of 2006 in Porto Alegre, Brazil[7] with the intent that at this later meeting a call to action might be produced. AGAPE in this context is not only a reference to the Greek word for the type of love that we are exhorted to display throughout the New Testament, it is an acronym standing for Alternative Globalization Addressing Peoples and Earth.

The AGAPE Background Document defines neoliberalism as the ideology that underlies, promotes, and seeks to legitimize concentration of multifaceted power structures.[8] Ironically, this concentration of power, leadership and decision making ability is in opposition to the democracy that the leading national powers in the globalized community often preach.

The major problem with neoliberalism is wonderfully stated in the AGAPE Background Document;

"(Neoliberalism) drives neoliberal capitalism and neoliberal globalization. In this perspective, neoliberalism provides an ideological cloak for the project of economic globalization that expands power and domination through an interlocking web of international institutions, national policies, corporate and investor practices and individual behavior. In essence, neoliberalism turns human beings into commodities and reduces the role of national governments to secure harmonious and sustainable social development. It places the utmost emphasis on capital and so-called "unfettered markets" to allocate resources and to promote growth.[9]"

Benjamin Valentin's tremendous work, *Mapping Public Theology: Beyond Culture Identity and Difference*, says that within neoliberalism humans are "self-made and self-dependent individuals who exist ontologically prior to society and to their relationships to others.[10]" He goes on to say that in a society comprised of individuals operating from within this neoliberal paradigm "(citizens come) to an understanding of politics as merely a matter of protecting and maximizing individual interests.[11]"

It might be wise to next attempt to define capitalism, as it is the economic manifestation or vehicle of neoliberalism. Many attempts to define capitalism begin with a reference to German economic theorist, Max Weber. The same shall be true here. Within his often cited book *The Protestant Ethic and the Spirit of Capitalism*, he states that "A capitalist economic action (is) one which rests on the expectation of profit by the utilization of opportunities for exchange" involving the " rational capitalistic organization of (formally) free labor.[12]"

Valentin, describes capitalism not only as an economic system, but as a cultural system as well. Here is the best way to view capitalism's connection with neoliberalism—for it is a cultural movement that "has managed to weaken our social ability to cultivate non-market values such as love, care, service, commitment, friendship, solidarity, spirituality, and justice.[13] Capitalism is far more than an economic system. It is a neoliberal cultural lifestyle that has moved to so many of us through out the world with mass appeal.

Capitalism may not be an evil in itself, just as a nation like the U.S. (the buildings and streets of it) may not be evil. Rather it is the people, or the zeitgeist, or the sin of the people that might make a nation into a tool for unholy, selfish, and/or malicious purposes. In the same way capitalism is not bad, yet the way that it is used and perhaps even set up, can only have destructive results for the majority and a profiting growth for a very small minority—and this can have evil (non-God glorifying and destructive) results. The globalization of society has taken the unquenchable thirst for the growth of private capital that once only had very local effects, to a world wide scale. The economic game that corporations play to make a profit (adjustment of prices, wages, etc) once only affected the "lower class" workers of the certain area where a corporation existed. Today, the thirst for more profit has led large corporations, like the very often targeted Wal-Mart, to seek workers and products from around the world, thus affecting other markets/nations with draconian results. Now on a global scale the old form of capitalism plays out with those in power (owners of the corporations) getting wealthier, and the workers working at manipulated wages, the local small business owners who cannot compete with low prices, and the workers back home who cannot work for the low wages that workers of neighboring countries can, all get poorer.

Within neoliberal globalization, capitalism has had devastating effects on our world. The AGAPE Background Document testifies as to how today 1.5 Billion people in the world, mostly women and children and Indigenous Peoples, live on less than one dollar a day. This is while the world's wealthiest 20% account for 86 percent of the global consumption of goods and services. The document states that "The annual income of the richest 1% is equal to that of the poorest 57% and at least 24,000 people die every day from poverty and malnutrition.[14]"

In the *State of Black America 2005*, the annual report by The Urban League, the effects of capitalism are described particularly with Black Americans in mind. This document describes how in 2005 Black unemployment remained at 10.8% while white unemployment decreased to 4.7% making Black unemployment 2.3 times more than whites. Regarding home ownership—the home-ownership rate for blacks was nearly 50% as opposed to more than 70% for whites. Further, Blacks are denied mortgage and home improvement loans at twice the rate of whites. Major disparities in average income, education rates, health, and criminal justice are all also given appropriate attention within the report.[15]

Scholar/Activist Manning Marable says in his classic *How Capitalism Underdeveloped Black America*, "I remain convinced that Black people as a group will never achieve the historical objectives of their long struggle for freedom within the political economy of capitalism." He goes on to say that while capitalism has demonstrated the uncanny ability to "mutate into various social formations and types of state rule . . . its essentially oppressive character, grounded in the continuing dynamics of capital accumulations and the exploitation of labor, remains the same.[16]"

The U.S. Census Bureau Press Release regarding Poverty Statistics,[17] attests to the terrible lot that African Americans have faced in a capitalist United States. Between 2003 and 2004 the median household income remained unchanged at $44,389. The median income for Black Households was $30, 134, the lowest among ethnic groups. Further, the nations official poverty rate rose from 12.5% in 2003 to 12.7 percent in 2004. There were 37.0 Million people living in poverty (decided by a suspect poverty threshold) with again, Blacks having the largest percentage at 24.7.

Other statistics pointing out how Blacks make up the highest percentage of the homeless, have terrible high school dropout rates, and make up a horrendous percentage of those that are incarcerated, could be shared. All of these are connected to the capitalism that is beating so many in our world down-especially Blacks.

As the above statistics demonstrate, poverty is a complex state of existence which encompasses far more than a lack of financial resources. The following section will consider more the predominant theories on the origins and sustenance of poverty rather than a linguistic definition.

Dr. Michael Katz in his book *The Underserving Poor*, describes how poverty is far more than not having money. He describes how poverty is the inability to enjoy/benefit from all that a society has to offer. He demonstrates how a number of failings and withdrawls by the government have resulted in the poverty of many of our citizens.

One of the origins/causes of poverty, he argues is that there is a lack of adequately paying jobs. In his book *One Nation, Underprivileged* Dr. Mark Rank explains that not only are there not enough jobs (as demonstrated by constant unemployment rates) but that there are not enough jobs that pay "a living wage.[18]" jobs that only pay a minimum wage ($5.15) ends up giving only about $800 a month. He describes how the average rent for a two-bedroom apartment across metropolitan areas is $600. This leaves $200 to spend on other necessities (clothing, food, child care, etc.) It is easy to see what a lack of jobs contribute to poverty.

Another systemic reason put forth is a lack of affordable housing. This is of course connected to the lack of jobs argument as people can not afford to live in certain areas—especially areas where there are the most jobs. The result is people have to live further out, pay for public transportation, gas and travel.

Rank also speaks about the "uneven playing field" that the U.S. is. He uses the brilliant example of a Monopoly game where one player gets $5000. Another $1500, and another $250. He explains that many of those experiencing poverty start out there because, like wealth among the rich, poverty is often passed down through generations.[19]

Both Rank and Katz, outline other origins and causes of poverty including education discrepencies, lack of universal healthcare, and more. I would just add that Rank argues that there are not only systemic causes but that there are also cultural and ideological trends that poverty has also originated from. He talks about how the U.S. is a nation where individualism has been celebrated. This is not always bad as we have prized our "freedoms" to act as individuals. However, this has also resulted in a "me first" mentality.

Connected to this is the emphasis on self-reliance that has been putforth. Perhaps in greatest demonstration of this is Ben Franklin's famous quote God helps those who help themselves." Aside from being theologically questionable, this has helped to perpetuate the theory that the poor need to "help themselves.[20]"

With this has come the perpetuation of the myth of the American Dream. This is the notion that "with enough hard work and dedication, anyone can make it in America." This goes on to say that even hardship can be overcome with perserverance and work. This theory helps to take the blame off of others and the government and places the blame on the poor for being poor. And therein lies the difference of the two major theories of poverty—that it is the result of personal shortcomings/lack of action vs. the result of systemic issues, including but not limited to capitalism. At this point, this essay will return to its major question of how Black Christians have engage capitalism and poverty.

Capitalism as an economic system has not worked for most of the world and it certainly has not worked for blacks. By not working, I am referencing some of the statistics shared earlier demonstrating how so few in the world are wealthy and how so many are in poverty. The historic response of many Christian ministers in this nation in the face of systems that do not work has been to fight the oppressive power, to Let God speak through them prophetically, and to be proactive in the shaking down of dangerous walls. Why is it that rather than fight this current juggernaut of an enemy, many ministers find themselves working for ways to participate and to capitalize off of it?

On the 27th of June 2006, a number of ministers and scholars gathered at Friendship-West Baptist Church in Dallas Texas for The National Conference and Revival for Social Justice in the Black Church. There panelists and participants spoke out against what they described as the Prosperity Gospel that is being preached in so many of our churches. This prosperity gospel is also known as the Word of Faith Gospel of the Gospel of Wealth and Self-Help.

"The message of many churches has been co-opted by American capitalism," said the Rev. Frederick Haynes III of the Friendship-West Baptist Church in South Dallas. "A megachurch should not just be known for the traffic jam it creates on Sunday, but for doing something more in the community."

Haynes and a number of the other ministers and theologians present including Rev. Jesse Jackson, were confronting Pastors, especially Black Pastors of megachurches for only preaching messages that deal with increasing the wealth of their congregants or bettering their situations in life. The conference/revival participants believed that rather than be so inwardly focused, ministers and their churches need to be addressing issues related to social justice.

One of the pastors called out by name was Bishop T.D. Jakes of The Potter's House also based in Dallas. More than 30,000 congregants worship at The Potter's House and that number does not include the thousands that watch and hear Bishop Jakes on television and radio each day around the world. In response to the criticism he said that "Economic empowerment and family prosperity are crucial to our survival." He continues, "The economic gulf that exists between people of color . . . and European-Caucasians is a breach that remains too wide, a chasm that should and can be closed.[21]"

Bishop Jakes is right on when he speaks of the gulf, the breach, and the chasm being too wide. It is not the place of this essay to question the theological legitimacy of Bishop Jakes' preaching. Further, this author has been blessed by Bishop Jakes and his ministry. Still, even beyond critiquing the Prosperity Gospel Message theologically, strategically it is unwise and selfish.

Finding ways for a small group of individuals to gain wealth and power at the expense of others (a mandate in a capitalist system) will not bridge the gulf Bishop Jakes is talking about. There will still be a very large mass of poor people in the world and in the Black community. There will just be a few more people of color among the haves.

Before continuing, I should say that I do consider Bishop Jakes to be a very gifted and especially anointed man of God. I have had the great blessing to hear Bishop Jakes live. His ministry is profound and powerful and without question, people have come to know the Lord through his preaching and teaching. I praise God for that. Further, his work in prisons, and in the healing ministry have touched countless numbers of lives. Most recently he was appointed co-chair of the Interfaith Rebuilding Initiative (distributing funds raised by Former Presidents George H.W. Bush and Bill Clinton to aid those devastated by Hurricane Katrina and the lack of help they received.)

It goes without saying that Bishop Jakes has done, and is doing a wonderful amount of work on behalf of the poor, the oppressed, and the needy. But, his work, being done in a capitalist system and with a capitalist goal of the accumulation of more wealth for just a certain part of the population—could be much more effective and if adjusted, could contribute to the eradication of poverty, oppression and great need.

At the previously mentioned conference/revival in Dallas, one of the ministers present was Rev. Jesse Jackson of the RainbowPUSH Coalition. He was among the voices calling on Prosperity Gospel Ministers to be more socially conscious. Before bringing critique to Rev. Jackson's economic projects, it should be mentioned that few have worked for justice and equality not only in the U.S. but around the world, the way that Rev. Jackson has. For more than forty years, Rev. Jackson has been on the frontlines and God has certainly moved through him.

Yet, since his days of working with Dr. King in the Southern Christian Leadership Conference (SCLC), he has always been on the Right Wing of the struggle for economic equality. He has recognized the "unlevel playing field" that exists as far as Blacks are concerned, but rather than producing a revolutionary vision to repave this field that will always produce (Black) losers, he has in different ways suggested ways for a few Black players to be able to play the game somewhat successfully while the majority continue to suffer.

Chicago-based journalist Salim Muwakkil writes:

"In a world where, as a friend quips, 'the IMF and all the other MF's control the global economy' there seems to be little alternative but to learn the rules of capitalism. In the introduction to his new book, (Jesse) Jackson writes, "Failing to understand the role of money in a capitalist system is like being a fish that doesn't know how to navigate water.'"[22]

"Learning the rules of capitalism" is just what many of our ministers and theologians, including Jesse Jackson have done. Editor of the International Socialist Review Ahmed Shawki describes the "Black Capitalism" prescribed by Jackson through the Rainbow PUSH coalition as "Emphasized support for Black Businesses, self reliance and the development of conservative mores within the Black Community."[23]

Again, Rev. Jackson has demonstrated a commitment to fighting oppression, particularly economic oppression against Blacks and people of color. Yet, his liberating projects are among the most capitalist proposed by any national Black leader. His goals of creating black millionaires and *Fortune 500* Black Businesses come with a price. That price is on the backs of others, mostly other Blacks that will be making those millionaires and Great Businesses through their labor, spending power, low wages, and struggle. Having a few Black faces in the pages of *Forbes Magazine* or a few more Black faces in the board room (as important accomplishments as they may be) will not solve the problem of an increasing amount of Black poverty and Black Joblessness.

A survey of the history of Capitalism in this young nation and throughout the world, will reveal that as a system, it cannot work for the majority of people because of the nature of the way it is set up. Certainly sin plays a role in the greed and lack of sharing resources that exists through out our society, but the way a capitalist political economy is set up, profit is the goal and profit comes at the expense of others. While being far from perfect in any of it diverse forms, socialism has stood as the major political/economic alternative to capitalism. The remainder of this essay will consider why African Americans and especially African American ministers should embrace, or at least become allied with a socialist movement of resistance and revolution.

"TO BE BLACK AND A SOCIALIST IN AMERICA IS TO BE NONCONFORMIST." —MANNING MARABLE *HOW CAPITALISM UNDERDEVEOLPED BLACK AMERICA*[24]

While small in number, there is a rich history of Black Socialists in this nation, with many of them being clergy and church people. Most Marxist historians trace the advent of Marxism in the United States to the early 1850's when Joseph Weydemeyer, "a comrade and friend of Karl Marx and Frederick Engels" immigrated to this nation.[25] He is described as the most important Marxist propagandist in the U.S. at that time. Though it should be noted that there were socialist and utopian groups in the country as early as the decades leading up to the Civil War. These Utopian socialists were the major type of socialism in the U.S. through their intentional communities that were spread throughout the Midwest and West.[26]

The Utopian socialists and the Marxist socialists, while agreeing on some basic economic and political tenants, found themselves at odds on many other key issues, including the question of slavery and the place that Blacks should have in American society. One of the more progressive socialist groups of the time was the Communist Club of New York which invited and encouraged Blacks to become members.

It is not until around 1879 that Blacks began to actively support and join socialist parties in any major numbers. One of the first Black men to publicly identify himself with socialism was Peter Clark. A local organizer in St. Louis, he would later become the first Black to hold a position of leadership in a Socialist Party in this nation.

While different socialist parties showed sympathy and even action toward abolition and then various civil rights, it was through the American Communist Party(s) that the most pro-Black action was taken. After the Russian Revolution, Communism emerged not only as the dominant socialist movement, but also as a growing world political system. Therefore, many of the American Communist (formally Socialist Party) Party's positions would come from Russia. It was not immediately that the International Communist leadership (Comintern) spoke on what they called "The Negro question." Yet, after the Forth (International) Congress of the Comintern held in 1922, they released the following "Theses of the Negro Question."

"Therefore the congress recognizes the necessity of supporting every form of the Negro movement which undermines or weakens capitalism, or hampers its further penetration.

The Communist International will use every means at its disposal to force that trade unions admit Black workers, or, where this right already exists on paper, to conduct special propaganda for the entry of Negroes into unions. If this should prove impossible, the Communist International will organize the Negroes in trade unions of their own and use united front tactics to compel their admission.

The Communist International will take steps immediately to convene a world Negro congress or conference."[27]

The number of Black members of the Communist Party did not rise dramatically just yet, but these public steps in solidarity with Blacks did manage to attract many members of a very important Black Nationalist Marxist group—The African Blood Brotherhood.

Organized in 1919 by Cryril Briggs, Richard Moore, and W.A. Domingo, the ABB had only about 12 years of existence though it fostered large chapters in New York, Chicago, Baltimore, Omaha, West Virginia, Trinidad, Surinam, British Guiana, Santo Domingo, and the Winward Islands. In *Black Marxism* scholar Cedric Robinson presents a list of other important Black Radicals that were members of the ABB movement, including Otto Huiswoud, Otto Hall, Haywood Hall (Harry Haywood), Edward Doty, Grace Campbell, H.V. Phillips, Gordon Owens, Alonzo Isable, and Lovett Fort-Whiteman.[28]

Theodore Vincent in his book *Black Power and The Garvey Movement* (ramparts, San Fran 1972) says that "The ABB saw itself as a tight-knit, semi-clandestine, paramilitary group which hoped to act for a worldwide federation of Black organizations . . . in order to build a strong and effective movement on the platform of liberation for the Negro people."[29]

The ABB is an organization whose full story remains to be told. Their relationship with Marcus Garvey and the Universal Negro Improvement Association, as well as their relationship with the Communist Party USA are complex and probably too tangential for this short piece. But for the purposes of this essay, it will suffice to say that the ABB was perhaps the earliest Black Liberation group that embraced Marxism, thus paving the way for later such groups like the Black Panthers.

As the ABB began to decrease in size and activity, many of the members moved into the CPUSA. This movement was after failed attempts to pull the UNIA over to more of a socialist outlook. The presence of Blacks in the CPUSA would continue to grow slowly throughout the1920's. After the famous "Black Belt Theory" more Blacks would enter the party paving the way for the unprecedented growth of Blacks in the CPUSA during the 1930's. Ahmed Shawki describes the Black Belt theory by saying "At its sixth congress in 1928, the Comintern declared that southern Blacks in the U.S. constituted a nation and that the party should adopt the slogan of "Self determination in the Black Belt" for party work among Blacks."[30]

This as well as their work during the Scottsboro trial, would make the CPUSA into a strong force among Blacks. In 1930 there were just less than 1000 Black members in the CPUSA. This number grew to 5005 in 1939.[31]

The coming years would see a number of famous Black women and men enter the Communist Party or at least sympathize with them (which meant being labeled Communist anyway). Among them were, authors Richard Wright, Claude McKay, Langston Hughes, Ralph Elliston, Chester Himes, some years later, Paul Robeson (who never officially joined the party, but offered to join and remained supportive) and W.E.B. DuBois. DuBois, as is the case in so many aspects of Black History serves as the great bridge between the Black socialists of the early 1900's and the Black Power socialists of the 1960's and 70's., and other Black socialists of the last part of the century.

Of the many biographies that have been written about Dr. DuBois, Manning Marable's *W.E.B. DuBois Black Radical Democrat* perhaps best describes the praxis of his work. DuBois, who did not officially join the Communist Party until 1961 (only two years before he died at age 95), showed interest and sympathy for socialism very early into his career.[32] No other Black writer has had greater influence on Blacks worldwide over the last century plus.

His passing on the eve of the March on Washington gave way to a new generation of Black radicals in the U.S. There were two major strands of Black socialism that the 1960's bore in the U.S.—the Black Nationalist Socialism expressed by Angela Davis and other Black Panther types, and the Democratic Socialism whispered by others like Martin Luther King Jr.

Founded in 1966, by Richard Aoki, Bobby Seale and Huey Newton, the organization originally known as The Black Panther Party for Self-Defense, would move from being strictly a Black Nationalist group to a legitimately socialist one. The Panthers while being best known for the clothes they wore and the arms they legally displayed, did far more than they are often recognized for. Many local and national anti-poverty programs were initiated ranging from day care and education projects to food distribution. Some famous Black Panthers were, Angela Davis, Assata Shakur, Afeni Shakur, H. Rap Brown, Stokely Carmichael, Mumia Abu-Jamal, Fred Hampton, and Geronimo Pratt.

Was Rev. Martin Luther King Jr. a socialist? Have there been any Black ministers who were also socialists? Before answering the first question, a brief history of Black Christian Socialists should be reviewed.

In 1896 Reverdy C. Ransom, a man who would go on later to become a Bishop in the AME Church, wrote "The Negro and Socialism" a piece he would advocate socialism in.[33] Within this article Ransom said when the "Negro comes to realize that socialism offers him freedom of opportunity to cooperate with all people upon terms of equality in every avenue of life, he will not be slow to accept his social emancipation."[34]

Some other Black ministers that advocated socialism in writing near the turn of the previous century were Bishop James T. Holly ("Socialism from the Biblical Point of View"[35]) and George F. Miller ("Enslavement of the Worker"[36] and "Socialism and Its Ethical Basis"[37]).

Rev. George Washington Woodbey would emerge onto the national socialist stage as the sole Black delegate to the 1904 and 1908 conventions of the

Socialist Party. Woodbey was a Baptist minister from San Diego, California and was a contributor to *The Christian Socialist*. A former slave freed after the civil war, he would become one of the most consistent Black Christian Socialist voices this nation would hear.[38] At one point he was even nominated to be Eugene Debs' running mate at one of the conventions though the nomination was turned down.

As Dr. Cone correctly states in his often forgotten article "The Black Church and Marxism: What do they have to say to Each Other?", "Black socialists are invisible in the histories of socialism written by white intellectuals."[39] That being the case, then the history of Black Christian socialists will prove even more difficult to uncover.

And so in the latter half of the 20th century and in the beginnings of the 21st, have many Black Christian Socialist ministers emerged? To this James Cone says:

> "The same (indifference) is true of Black preachers and theologians today. They are indifferent toward socialism, because they know little about it and because they believe that the reality of racism is too serious to risk dilution with socialism. When one reads the histories of the Black churches in the works of Joseph Washington, Carter G. Woodson, E. Franklin Frazier, Gayraud S. Wilmore and others, it is revealing that there are no references to Black socialist preachers."[40]

That quote by Cone is from 1980 and was very applicable back then on the eve of the Cold War and with major socialist and communist powers in the world. Socialism was a possibility or at least it was in the vocabulary of more ministers than today. Cone retells the story of what he calls the one event that presented the radical Black church movement of the 1960's with an opportunity "to consider the Marxist question.

"(This was) when James Forman issued "The Black Manifesto" in Riverside Church May 4, 1969. While the National Conference of Black Churchmen supported Forman, their support ignored the "Introduction" of the Manifesto because it was Marxist. The Black preachers of NCBC strongly endorsed the demands of the Manifesto. However, they sidestepped the Marxist justification of the demands, using instead their own nationalist arguments. While James Forman was referred to as a modern-day prophet by NCBC and other Black church people, no Black church person, to my knowledge, endorsed his perspective on Marxism. In fact, during all the discussions I attended on the Manifesto issue, no one even raised the issue of Marxism."[41]

Before moving to the present, the question of Martin King's socialist leanings should be addressed. Like DuBois, numerous biographies and articles have been written about King. Every year during the celebration of his Birthday and the National Holiday in his honor, commercials appear with sound and video bites replaying the famous "I have a dream" speech. Yet, in so many of these books, articles, celebratory observances, and TV clips, very few ever mention King's commitment to economic justice let alone his relationship with socialism.

In a speech at Brown University on February 2nd 2007, Dr. Cornel West describes what young Coretta Scott wrote in her journal about meeting her future husband in her journal saying that "it was the first time she ever met a Black Democratic Socialist." Cornel goes on to describe how Martin at that point was already a member of the Intercollegiate Socialist Society.

Once again, turning to James Cone will bring some enlightenment to this subject. In his magnificent work *Martin & Malcolm & America: A Dream or a Nightmare*, Cone explores the socialist leanings of both Malcolm and Martin towards the end of their lives. In regards to Martin he says:

"Unlike Malcolm who did not have an opportunity to read Marx, Martin read him 'during the Christmas holidays of 1949'.He spoke of his 'anti-capitalist feelings' in a paper he wrote at Crozer Seminary, and his wife Coretta, observed the same sentiment in the 1950's. Although he admired Marx's 'great passion' for social justice,' it was not until he went to Sweden that he began to consider a European version of socialism as an alternative to American Capitalism. 'I am always amazed when I go there,' Martin said of Sweden. 'They don't have any poverty. No unemployment, nobody needing health services can't get them. They don't have any slums. The question is why. It is because Scandinavia has grappled with the problem of a more equitable distribution of wealth'

Because he was still deeply aware of the harm that a communist smear could do to the civil rights movement, he was very cautious about the dangers of speaking too positively of democratic socialism."[42]

Cone goes on to say;

"During staff retreats, he often requested that the tape recorders be switched off, so he could express his views frankly and honestly about the need for a complete, revolutionary change in the American political economy, replacing capitalism with some form of socialism."[43]

What should we do with this? Is Cone just spinning Martin to make him fit into his own political leanings? Was this just an intellectual interest of Martin's or was he sincerely a closet socialist? How might his ministry have continued had he not died that terribly sad April Day almost four decades ago? Well, he did die while in the midst of a campaign for the rights of Sanitation Workers in Memphis.

Today, Black Socialists seem to be experiencing a resurgence. A number of well known scholars, theologians, and activists are once again presenting themselves as socialists, most notably, Dr. Cornel West who describes himself as a "Non-Marxist democratic socialist." West has consistently personified the model of Christian and Scholar/Activist. His writings, which transcend philosophical, theological, and sociological fields, have been consistently striking a blow for justice. Works like *Black Theology and Marxist Thought* (1979), *Prophesy Deliverance* (1982), *Breaking Bread* (1991), *The Ethical Dimensions of Marxist Thought* (1991), *Race Matters* (1993), *The Future of American Progressivism* (1998) and *Democracy Matters* (2004) have all been both national bestsellers as well as convicting pieces of literature. As a professor at Union Seminary, Harvard University and most recently Princeton University, he has been challenging students to think critically about the economic and political system they are living in. And as an activist, he ha made appearances and given speeches everywhere from the Million Man March and Millions More Movement to the State of the Black Church meetings sponsored by Tavis Smily. Further he has been involved in the presidential campaigns of Bill Bradley and Rev. Al Sharpton. Certainly he is a model of praxis today. But we all can't have the same type of ministry as Dr. West. How then shall we be?

Before entering the final section of this paper, I can not help but ask the obvious question—"Who am I to propose any type of project that will encourage ministers (clergy and lay) to begin to take on neoliberal globalized capitalism?" I am just a twenty-something Hip Hop B-Boy who hopes and leans towards a democratic socialism stemming from interpretation of scripture. Yet, while holding these political/economic beliefs, I perpetuate the capitalist system everyday as I try, along with my wife, to raise my family. I fall short of the intellectual ideals that I put forth in regards to resisting conformity in this system and I certainly take advantage of the moderate, yet real, privileges that have been afforded to me.

Praise God for the grace! I call myself a Christian. Yet, it seems like every minute I fall short of being faithful to Christ. I sin literally all of the time, missing the mark. And while being a "disciplined socialist" does not hold nearly the same import as being faithful to our Lord Jesus, I suppose the correlation is that we need not be perfect. In the case of Christianity, there is grace. In the case of searching for alternatives to capitalism and pursuing socialism—we are in process, working toward the goal politically and personally.

Thus far, this almost motley essay has endeavored to describe the crisis that global capitalism has brought to our society, to describe the history of its primary intellectual and political alternative here in the United States among African Americans, and then to trace the thin, but relevant history of socialism among Black Ministers here in the U.S.

Now this essay asks the question, how can we encourage ministers, both clergy and lay, to be more socially conscious around socio-economic and political issues? In the context of this paper, that question is really, How can we get ministers to think critically rather than opportunistically about capitalism?

Perhaps the first place to begin is at our seminaries and Bible Colleges that are preparing women and men for various forms of ministry. More and more, courses dealing with "Church and Society" are being taught all around the country. Many of these courses, like those taught by Proessor. Katie Day at Lutheran Theological Seminary of Philadelphia, challenge and equip ministers to partner with their neighbors and to be conscious of "social justice issues." This is so important. Yet, these types of classes can go a step further. With Professor Day being at the better end of the spectrum, most courses hold off on encouraging ministers to think critically about economic issues on a systemic scale. Sure, they think about the homeless or ways to serve the poor, but very seldom do they ask students to examine the ways our political/economic system may or may not be a healthy one. While there are certain courses and professors that break the norm like Prof. Day's courses or Prof. Larry Rasmussen's (formerly of Union Seminary in New York) classes that consider alternatives to capitalism, the majority (and on this I speak from only my personal experience in seminary and visiting many seminaries) remain silent on this topic. Professors, regardless of what they think about capitalism and socialism, can be challenged to think about economic and political issues and to consider ways their specialties interlock with them.

Another front this battle can be fought on is through the denominational offices. It would not be impossible to formulate (some have already been) economic studies that denominations could distribute to their churches and constituents. These Bible study/workshops would not be meant to create socialists or necessarily anti-capitalists, but rather to get Christians to think for themselves with the facts laid out fairly before them. Understanding, rather than conversion is the goal of this endeavor.

It may seem that socialism or some pre-capitalist form of feudalism, are the only alternatives to capitalism and the globalized capitalism that much of our world finds itself navigating through. Yet, there have been some other alternatives that have been proposed and even established over the last several years. While the various forms of socialism mostly emerge from spaces outside of the church and the Christian tradition, the next section of this essay will consider alternatives that have been proposed and in some cases acted upon, from within the Body of Christ and its heritage.

Within the AGAPE Background Document, its authors suggest that churches and established church collectives begin to embrace and embody liberating methods which might help them and their congregants to break free from the "death dealing paradigm of Neoliberal Globalization." In other words, they are suggesting that churches demonstrate and live out alternatives themselves. This is the church as a community of alternatives. An example of this is a denomination divesting from businesses or corporations that exploit employees, nations and the environment. Some might say that denominations need to divest from all capital growing activities and rather invest in humans via schools and other potentially life giving community development enterprises.

Along with serving as models and real examples of alternatives, churches and church collectives[44] can lift up and acknowledge smaller efforts to combat the destructive side of globalized capitalism. Throughout the AGAPE Background Document, the authors identify alternative enterprises around the world. One such "lifted up" effort is an agrochemical enterprise in Sao Paulo, Brazil. They describe how at a moment of high indebtedness, the company "started investing funds and time in its own cadre of employees . . . (with some) innovations including improvements in remuneration, the creation of indirect forms of remunerations, time for studying during the work year, and encouragement to cooperate rather than compete in the work environment." Soon the company's financial situation was much improved and the company continued to invest in its employees and the surrounding community through initiatives like the building of a community school and a new "two-pronged policy of profit-sharing and democratization of the stocks."[45] This is a wonderful example of a positive enterprise being held up by a larger church body.

Lastly, churches and church bodies can work toward either the changing of policy or the socializing of various part of society (education, travel, medicine and other aspects). The various denominations, collectives, and some individual churches, may hold influence locally, nationally, and internationally—influence that might be able to effect changes in policy. This would indeed be a strong way for the church to respond to the painful side of neoliberal globalization.

Along with alternatives coming forth from churches and the actions of churches, strong alternatives to globalized capitalism can and have emerged from the Bible. In a class lecture, Dr. Larry Rasmussen said that. "(The church) has lost the radical Christian tradition (which included) Jubilee, Sabbath not only for humans, but for the land, and many other alternatives."[46] Full volumes could be written on alternatives that might come forth from the Bible, but one brief alternative that the late theologian John Howard Yoder puts forth comes from the life and words of Jesus Christ.

In his powerful book *The Politics of Jesus*, Yoder attempts to as he says, ". . . throw a cable across the chasm which usually separates the disciplines of New Testament exegesis and contemporary social ethics." The author challenges us to take the radical nature of Jesus as displayed in the Gospels, seriously. Jesus' teachings and actions around issues such as wealth / (re)distribution of wealth, revolutionary restructuring of power, being servants to one another and non-violence are political statements that are very different from the mainstream of today, he argues. As Christians we are to be followers of Him whose name we bear. Therefore, we should also be revolutionarily political and follow Him in name and in deed. A not so subtle subtext of the book is the need for pacifism and non-violent pro-action by believers.

One specific alternative that Yoder puts forth is a reconsideration of what is known as "The Lord's Prayer." He focuses on what might need to be a retranslation of the section that is translated often as "Forgive us our trespasses, as we forgive those who have trespassed against us." In some places it might be translated as "Forgive us our debts as we forgive our debtors."[47] Yoder states that this verse would best be translated at "Forgive us our debts, as we forgive those that owe us debts." This Biblical calling for debt forgiveness, if embraced, would put a massive dent in the machine of neoliberal globalization as the collection of loans with interest is a part of the paralyzing work of the World Bank and other international financial entities. The presentation of debt forgiveness as a Biblical notion is a wonderful alternative from within the Christian Tradition.

Another alternative model might come forth from The Holy Trinity as described by theologian Leonardo Boff. Boff does not withhold criticism for either capitalism nor socialism. Yet he does more than critique, he also provides (holds up) a tremendous alternative.

Boff believes that it is not capitalism nor is it socialism that holds the answer for a successful economic/political system where all, including the poor can have the opportunity to live to their fullest potential. It is in a system modeled on the Triune communion. It is easy to project onto the Trinitarian Community some of the traits of capitalism and socialism (upholding the individual personhood, yet fully sharing life), yet there are real lessons that might be learned from observation of The Three.

"There is a fundamental human yearning for sharing, equality, respect for differences, and communion of all with God. The communion of the Divine Three offers a source of Inspiration for achieving these age-old yearnings of all people and all societies. Each Divine person shares fully in the other two: in life, love, and communion. Each is equal in eternity, majesty, and dignity; none is superior or inferior to the others. Although equal in sharing in life and love, each Person is distinct from the others . . . but this distinction allows for communion and mutual self-giving. The Persons are distinct so as to be able to give out of their wealth to the others and to form eternal communion and divine community. The Blessed Trinity is the most wonderful community."[48]

It might be easier to fall into a position of criticism when placing the Trinity next to the two economic systems discussed here, however it is better to see the "Trinitarian Communion (as) a source of inspiration."[49]

Boff was and is not the only Theologian to see a connection between the Trinity and the way we as societies live out our collective lives here on Earth. He quotes noted theological scholar Jurgen Moltmann as saying;

> "Only a Christian community that is whole, united, and unifying, free of dominion and oppression, and only a humanity that is whole, united and unifying, free of class domination and dictatorial oppression, can claim to respect the Trinitarian God. This is a world in which human beings are characterized by their social relationships and not by their power and possessions. This is a world in which human beings hold everything in common and share everything, except their personal characteristics."[50]

The Holy Trinity serves as another, perhaps the ideal, model for an alternative society. Yet, as we hold up the Trinity as our model, we continue to search for ways to arrive at the Trinitarian Societal model. Another such alternative may be found in the Focolare Movement.

During World War II, Chiara Lubich and several other young women in Trent, Italy formed a small religious community that was based on scriptural teachings about faithfulness to God and faithfulness to our neighbors. As their website says, "From its humble beginnings . . . the Focolare has become a worldwide movement, and now numbers over 87,000 members and about two million friends and adherents in over 180 nations"[51] reflecting an ecumenically diverse composition. Chiara Lubich has become an internationally known figure and during her life has received the Templeton Prize for Progress in Religion (1977) as well as the Augsburg Peace Prize (1988). Her, and the main goal of the movement along with being faithful to God, is the unity of humankind.

One of the initiatives of the Focolare Movement that is working towards this unity is the "Economy of Communion Project." Initialized in 1991 by Chiara Lubich while on her way to a visit in Sao Paulo, Brazil. The project challenges business leaders (within and outside of the Focolare Movement) to follow three specific guidelines.

"Businesses will freely put their profits in common just as the early Christian communities did. First, they will help those in need financially, or offer them a job, taking action so that no one remains in need. (Second) they will also reinvest part of their profits in the business and (third) use a portion to develop the structures of the little cities of the Focolare Movement where people will learn how to live and work in a culture of giving."[52]

Lubich says that the "Economy of Communion came into existence to reach a day when we will be able to give an example of a people where no one is in need, where no one is poor."[53] Through her Economy of Communion, Chiara Lubich and the Focolare Movement are providing a very strong alternative to neoliberal globalization/globalized capitalism.

Alternative economic structures and models are some of the powerful contributions to this conversation coming from the theological community. Along with the economy of communion, another such alternative economy is the "Theological Economy of Grace" described by theologian Kathryn Tanner. Tanner is the Dorothy Grant Maclear Professor of Theology in the Divinity School at the University of Chicago. Some of her previous books include, *God and Creation and Christian Theology*, *The Politics of God*, *Theories of Culture: A New Agenda for Theology*, and *Jesus, Humanity and the Trinity*. Within her succinct, yet powerful book *Economy of Grace*, Tanner "Tries to use a theological economy to expand our economic imaginations as far as possible."[54] She goes on to say;

> "That mean(s) rereading the Christian Story in ways that would allow for the greatest possible contrast between the principles of theological economy and those of capitalist exchange. . . . Theological economy on my understanding of it appears to have nothing to do with the present structures of global capitalism and therefore to be offering a utopia."[55]

Therefore, with her theological economy having nothing to do with global capitalism, she sees her proposed alternative economy as "germinating and flowering on alien soil" or "coming to life within the belly of the best" as opposed to coming from outside of the system or waiting for capitalism to destroy itself. In other words, she sees her proposed alternative as working within neoliberal globalization and bringing about change from the inside.[56]

Just what is that alternative economy that Tanner proposes? She calls for an Economy of Grace which is comprised of three simple yet profound adaptations from the Bible and the Trinity. The first is unconditional giving—just as the earth and all of creation was unconditionally given to us. This stands in direct tension with our current debt and interest practices that are employed in global capitalism. The second adaptation is Universal giving—just as God has pour out his love and given to all inhabitants of the Earth without discrimination, so should we share universally. This in Tanner's explanation translates into a common possession right and an obligation to share and give.

Lastly, she calls for "Noncompetition in a community of mutual benefit." This she describes as "First, there is no competition in property or possession . . . second there is no competition between having oneself and giving to others . . . and (third) (one's) having is not at any one else expense; to the contrary, it enables my giving to them for their good."[57] This proposal for a Theological Economy of Grace by Kathryn Tanner is a prime example of the kind of work and the kind of critical public theology that theologians can and should be doing.

Thank God for the alternatives described here as well as the many other alternatives that were not mentioned from the small commune like church communities such as the Sojourners to the centuries old monastic communities that have stood as alternatives since even before the emergence of capitalism. Yet, in order for these alternatives to continue and for other ones to come forth, God will continue to inspire people to develop movements like the Focolare movement, and theologians and church leaders will need to awaken to a critical consciousness of neoliberal globalization so that a real public theological engagement might take place. It is imperative that church leaders and theologians be challenged to attain *conscientizacao*[58] around the issues discussed in this piece. Throughout the History of the Church and before that, Ancient Israel, there have always been prophets, teachers and ministers that have spoken out against "Babylon." It is my belief that the Babylon of our day is global capitalism/neoliberal globalization resulting in a deadly poverty. What shall be the churches response to this triumphant juggernaut that holds it and much of the rest of the world captive? The church, through its lay, ordained, and academic theologians must articulate the innate problems with the system we find ourselves within and then from there, continue to provide alternatives. After the provision of alternatives, be they socialist or not, the church, by grace must work to implement them, bring them to reality and as Bob Marley said, "Chant Down Babylon."

NOTES

1. Cone, James "The Black Church and Marxism: What do they have to say to each other?" (The Institute for Democratic Socialism 1980) This essay was written for the Democratic Socialist Organizing Committee's Seminar on "Religion, Socialism, and the Black Experience," held at Asbury United Methodist Church, Washington, D.C. April 9th 1980.

2. On August 20, 1619 a Dutch ship arrived at Jamestown. On board were 20 captured Africans, who were sold as slaves at Jamestown. The initial Blacks to arrive were considered indentured servants like many whites in similar circumstances. The Blacks were freed many years later when the terms of their servitude ended. http://www.multied.com/AfiricanAmerican/1stBlacks.html

3. For more on this movement within Social Christianity from Social Gospel to Christian Realism, to Liberation Theology, see Dorrien, Gary *Soul In Society* (Fortress Press, Minneapolis, MN 1995).

4. I chose "realities" as opposed to philosophies or economic theories (in regards to neo-liberal and capitalism) because they each transcend both of these words.

5. Justice, Peace, and Creation Team—World Council of Churches (Geneva 2005) AGAPE Background Document—Quote is from the Forward.

6. Barber, Benjamin "Jihad Vs. McWorld" (*The Atlantic Monthly* March 1992).

7. Justice, Peace, and Creation Team—World Council of Churches (Geneva 2005) AGAPE Background Document.

8. Ibid p. 3.

9. Ibid. p. 3.

10. Valentin, Benjamin *Mapping Public Theology: Beyond Culture, Identity, and Difference* (Trinity Press International, Harrisburg PA 2002) p. 92.

11. Ibid p. 93.

12. Weber, Max The Protestant Ethic and The Spirit of Capitalism (Charles Scribner's Sons—New York, NY 1958) pp. 17, 21.

13. Valentin, Benjamin *Mapping Public Theology: Beyond Culture, Identity, and Difference* (Trinity Press International, Harrisburg PA 2002) p. 98.

14. Justice, Peace, and Creation Team—World Council of Churches (Geneva 2005) AGAPE Background Document p. 9.

15. Executive Summary *State of Black America 2005*, National Urban League April 6th 2005.

16. Marable, Manning *How Capitalism Underdeveloped Black America* (South End Press Cambridge, MA 2000) In the Critical Reassessment p. xxxviii.

17. Released August 30th 2005. All stated statistics are for 2004.

18. Rank, Mark *One Nation, Underprivileged* (New York, NY Oxford University Press 2005) p. 50–60.

19. Ibid. p. 70.

20. Ibid. p. 12.

21. Associated Press "Black Leaders Blast Megachurches, Say They Ignore Social Justice" June 29th 2006.

22. Muwakkil,Salim "Jesse Jackson's New Crusade: It's All about the Benjamins," *In These Times*, March 20, 2000.

23. Shawki, Ahmed *Black Liberation and Socialism* (Haymarket Books, Chicago IL 2006) p. 224.

24. Marable, Manning *How Capitalism Underdeveloped Black America* (South End Press Cambridge, MA 2000) In the Critical Reassessment p. 1.

25. Shawki, Ahmed *Black Liberation and Socialism* (Haymarket Books, Chicago IL 2006) p. 110.

26. Ibid (110).

27. Degras, Jane *The Communist International, 1919–1943, Vol 1. 1914–1922* (New York: Oxford University Press, 1956) p. 401.

28. Robinson, Cedric *Black Marxism* (UNC Press, Chapel Hill, NC 1983) p. 216.

29. Vincent, Theodore *Black Power and The Garvey Movement* (Ramparts Press, San Francisco, CA 1972).

30. Shawki, Ahmed *Black Liberation and Socialism* (Haymarket Books, Chicago IL 2006) p. 137 and Robinson, Cedric *Black Marxism* (UNC Press, Chapel Hill, NC 1983) p. 216.

31. Vincent, Theodore *Black Power and The Garvey Movement* (Ramparts Press, San Francisco, CA 1972) p. 551–552.

32. Marable, Manning *W.E.B. DuBois: Black Radical Democrat* (Paradigm Publishers, Boulder CO 2004) p. 108 describes how as early as 1907, writing in *Horizon* DuBois was giving strong consideration to what was happening overseas in socialist movements.

33. Cone, James "The Black Church and Marxism: What do they have to say to each other?" (The Institute for Democratic Socialism 1980) This essay was written for the Democratic Socialist Organizing Committee's Seminar on "Religion, Socialism, and the Black Experience," held at Asbury United Methodist Church, Washington, D.C. April 9th 1980.

34. This quote was found in the James Cone article previously mentioned. He referenced Foner, Phillip *American Socialism and Black Americans: From the Age of Jackson to World War II* (Westport, Connecticut: Greenwood Press, 1977) p. 205.

35. Holly, James T. "Socialism From the Biblical Point of View" *The AME Church Review* Vol. 10 1984.

36. Miller, George F. "Enslavement of the Worker" *The Messenger*, Vol. II No. 7 July 1919.

37. Miller, George F. "Socialism and Its Ethical Basis" *The Messenger* Vol. II No. 7 July 1919.

38. Cort, John *Christian Socialism* (Orbis Books, Maryknoll, NY 1988) p. 256.

39. Cone, James "The Black Church and Marxism: What do they have to say to each other?" (The Institute for Democratic Socialism 1980) This essay was written for the Democratic Socialist Organizing Committee's Seminar on "Religion, Socialism, and the Black Experience," held at Asbury United Methodist Church, Washington, D.C. April 9th 1980.

40. Ibid. p. 4.

41. Ibid. p. 4.

42. Cone, James *Martin & Malcolm & America: A Dream or a Nightmare* (Orbis Books, Maryknoll, NY 1999) p. 285–286. Here Cone, is referencing King, Martin *Stride Towards Freedom* (Harper Publishing, San Francisco 1958) p. 92, King, Martin *Strength to Love* (Harper Collins, San Francisco 1977) p. 100 as well as Martin King's "Address to Staff at Retreat" 19th of November 1966 @ KCA.

43. Ibid.

44. By church collectives I do not just mean denominations, but also groups like the World Council of Churches, the National Council of Churches here in the U.S. and other like bodies.

45. Justice, Peace, and Creation Team—World Council of Churches (Geneva 2005) AGAPE Background Document pp 39–40.

46. This lecture was a part of the *Ecumenical Social Ethics* Course he offered in the Spring semester of 2006 at Lutheran Theological Seminary of Philadelphia.

47. Ibid.

48. Boff, Leonardo *Holy Trinity, Perfect Community* (Maryknoll, NY, Orbis Books, 1988) p. 64.

49. Ibid Boff 1988 p. 151.

50. Moltmann, Jurgen *"La Dotrina Sociale de la Trinita" Sulla Trinita* (Napels, 1982) p. 36 and *Concillium 177* (1985) p. 50–58.

51. http://www.rc.net/focolare/

52. http://www.edc-online.org/uk/storia.htm

53. http://www.edc-online.org/uk/storia.htm

54. Tanner, Kathryn *Economy of Grace*(Augsburg Fortress Press, Minneapolis, MN 2005) p. 87.

55. Ibid. p. 87.

56. Ibid. p. 89.

57. Ibid. p. 76.

58. Freire, Paolo *Pedagogy of the Oppressed* (Continuum Books, New York 1970) Conscientizacao is realized by one gaining a critical interpretation and a critical understanding of the world—as opposed to simply/exclusively receiving the "banking education system" deposits of interpretation and understanding from one's teachers.

Afterword

James Spady—2007

REFLECTIONS ON PERSISTENT
POVERTY IN A POST KATRINA ERA

"What kind of poverty might it be that can never be eased and what kind of wealth might it be that cannot be used to change this poverty?"

    . . . Gumira Ajidarma, author of "Children of the Sky"[1]

The Indonesian author, Gumira Ajidarma raises a pivotal question facing public policy makers, scholars and elected officials in the United States as well as those attempting to intervene in the daily tragedies facing far too many poor and homeless people. The question is a profound one, "what kind of poverty might it be that can never be eased?' The follow up question for those attempting to institute or effect changes for the better in the world around them becomes, 'what kind of wealth might it be that cannot be used to change this poverty?"

    What can we learn about race, class and equity as we reflect on the catastrophic devastation resulting from natural and man made disasters? What can be said about the presence of decaying corpses floating through the streets of a major American city at the beginning of the 21st century? Starving survivors and homeless residents, continue to believe in a society where persistent poverty among African Americans increases at alarming rates in cities and towns all over the United States. How long can they continue to have hope as they face deplorable conditions daily? What happens to deferred dreams of Black men, women and children left homeless in the aftermath of Hurricane Katrina? Why are there so few discussions about the political economy of development in arriving at what to do in this post Katrina era?

Dr. Edward Weisband, Distinguished Teaching Professor in the Department of Political Science at the State University of New York at Binghamton, notes the following in the introduction to his groundbreaking text, *Poverty Amidst Plenty: World Political Economy and Distributive Justice:* " Development economics is a subfield of the discipline of economics and thus upon the methods of assessing economies stricken by poverty. To accomplish its aims, developmental economics seeks to alter deplorable socioeconomic conditions by:

• fostering efficient use of domestic services
• promoting increases in levels of economic productivity
• accelerating economic growth as measured by rising levels of national income, domestic savings and internal investment.[2]

Can we seriously attempt to redress the gross negligence shown African Americans in New Orleans' 9th Ward before, during and after Katrina? How can the high levels of unemployment decrease? How can critical lack of housing and poor health conditions improve? What will enable this population to move from levels of subsistence to a higher ground, without focusing on development economic strategies in the city, state and region."

What kind of poverty might it be that can never be eased? Why are the dispersed survivors of such a horrific experience as Katrina not provided incentives to return to their homes? Does not this unfortunate practice raise fundamental social issues of equality and justice for poor black people? Spike Lee's recent documentary, "When the Levees Broke: A Requiem in Four Acts," (a four hour HBO doc) provides illuminating testimonies by Katrina survivors regarding acts of betrayal and humiliation. One sees evidence of both connection and disconnection, a traumatic past and a distant future, instances of memory and re-memory, at times a willingness to freely recollect and at other times absolute fear in expressing what they had become. New Orleans was both home and a tyranny of place. How would they create a future for themselves and family when they remained so divided on the traumatic and hallucinatory past they had inherited? Many of them had survived a war of aggression and colonization under a system of apartheid in the American south of their birth and now they were exploring new genres of expression as they tried desperately to establish new levels of normality for themselves and their loved ones. And like many survivors, these black people were working through the emotions of victims and survivors, countering official memories and sensory memory with multiple forms of silences and erasures. Weren't they really standing outside of the definition of the nation state described by that notable triumvirate, BLN? Death and historical terror in the land of their birth had reached such exaggerated states of abnormality as to force them in a state of surreality only imagined by Andre Breton. What kind of poverty might it be that can never be eased? What future would these African Americans have in the New New Orleans?

RE-BUILDING NEW ORLEANS' 9TH WARD AFTER DISASTER

In an exclusive interview with the distinguished Urban Planner and Designer, Jonathan Barnett, Professor of Practice, Penn Design and an associate with the firm, Wallace, Roberts and Todd, LLC, we are provided the following insight: "There are probably parts of the 9th Ward that you can't reconstruct and maybe you shouldn't. But that doesn't mean that people from the 9th Ward can't come back. And it doesn't mean that they shouldn't be compensated for what happened to their homes. . . . I don't know all of the answers on this point. Some of the pumps failed because the electricity failed. Some of the pumps had generators and they continued to work but there was so much water coming in that they couldn't handle it. Basically, the older the pumps were, the better they worked. The first pumps that were done by the great engineer who built the system, all pretty well held up. But the whole city shouldn't have been designed so that you had to pump Lake Pontchatrain back into Lake Pontchatrain. That's never going to work."[3]

BUILDING A BIGGER AND BETTER CITY

Professor Barnett rightly concludes: "If anybody was really serious about New Orleans needing those gates that would have been made a public issue a long time ago.

Members of Congress could have gone back and talked to their constituents and said the money is there from the federal government. There is blame to go around but I think the federal government is, in the end, responsible. They built the flood levees. What we learn now is that the design was not correct and that the construction was not done properly. You can't blame the maintenance for that either. The cause of this problem was bad design and bad construction and it needn't have happened. You would have had wind damage. It would have been bad but it wouldn't have been as bad as it is now. The problem has to be redressed. Many people in New Orleans were told that they didn't need flood insurance because they had the levees. Now it turns out that the flood walls were poorly designed and badly constructed. . . . The key thing is to build a big and better city, not a leaner and meaner city."[4]

STRANGE THINGS HAPPENING EVERY DAY

The African American gospel singer and pioneer rock guitarist, Sister Rosetta Tharpe used to sing a song with Marie Knight called, "Strange Things Happen Every Day." In many ways that song accurately describes what is happening in the lives of many poor black people who were left homeless in the aftermath of Hurricane Katrina. Strange. Outside of one's previous experience but conceivably a part of one's 'racial memory." Strange. Distant or reserved, both unusual and extraordinary. They'd known the meaning of Billie Holiday's "Strange Fruit." And when that strange wind started to blow it must have been a warning of stranger things to come. And when you've had a life of strange things happening every day there is a cumulative impact that hits you with the force of a West African harmattan. Strange. Many thousands gone. Blood in the lakes, streams and rivers. Bright red blood spread on those white magnolias. Bloods and Crips in the streets of this chaotic city. Red blood moving through the alleys and back streets leading to the Magnolia Housing Projects. DuBois enters the jagged cipha and captures the essence of this new New Orleans when he says, " How strange a land is this—how full of untold story, of tragedy and laughter, and the rich legacy of human life, shadowed with a tragic past and big with future promise." Headline in today's paper reads, " 750,000 Homeless in America." Strange things happen every day.

THE SOULS OF BLACK FOLK ENTER THE SOULS OF POOR PEOPLE: SHALL THE CIRCLE REMAIN UNBROKEN?

Turning to Chapter VIII of *The Souls of Black Folk*, "Of The Quest of the Golden Fleece," DuBois states, "It is easy for us to lose ourselves in details in endeavoring to grasp and comprehend the real condition of a mass of human beings. We often forget that each unit in the mass is a throbbing human soul."[5] When night falls on the City of Philadelphia remember the throbbing human souls in some land of tenacious terror and human error. Midnight in the deepest part of the American South and suddenly you are face to face with a young black man who survived both Katrina's surge and the streets of the North. Young Jeezy's " The Inspiration" plays loudly in the alluring streets of the dirty dirty, what will dictate the nature of your interaction? When you meet a woman struggling to be both American and Muslim, a Hip Hop centered being desperately trying to communicate with his parents, a dirt farmer praying for more rain, a stranger in this strange, strange land, just remember the words of an old wise man, Dr. William Edward Burghardt DuBois: " We often forget that each unit of the mass is a throbbing human soul."[6]

NOTES

1. Ajidarma, Gumira. 2007. "Children of the Sky," in Alane Salerno Mason and Dedi Felman, (eds.) Words WIthout Borders: The World Through The Eyes of Writers, An Anthology," New York, Anchor Books (A Division of Random House, Inc.).

2. Westfield, Edward (ed.), 1989. Poverty Amidst Plenty: World Political Economy and Distributive Justice, Boulder, Colorado, Westview Press.

3. Jonathan Barnett, Interview with James G. Spady, 3 February, 2006.

4. Ibid.

5. DuBois, W. E. B., 2003, The Souls of Black Folk, New York, 44.

6. Ibid.

Contributors

Dennis Culhane, PhD is Professor of Social Welfare Policy in the School of Social Work and Professor of Psychology in Psychiatry in the School of Medicine at the University of Pennsylvania. He is also the faculty Director of the Cartographic Modeling Laboratory. He is the Senior Fellow at the Leonard Davis Institute of Health Economics as well as the Faculty Associate at the Center for Population Studies. Dr. Culhane's primary area of research is homelessness and housing distress. His current work includes studies of the impact of homelessness and supportive housing on the utilization of publicly funded health and human services in New York City. His recent research includes a study of the rates of homelessness by various subpopulations in eight US cities. Dr. Culhane's recent publications include studies of the housing and neighborhood factors related to the distribution of homeless persons' prior addresses in New York, Philadelphia and Washington, DC. Dr. Culhane is currently leading an effort to integrate property, neighborhood, and human services data from Philadelphia into several web-based geographic information system applications to support policy analysis, program planning and evaluation.

James Spady is a recipient of the American Book Award and the National Newspaper Association's Meritorious Award. His works have appeared in newspapers, magazines, scholarly journals, encyclopedias, and on radio, TV and film in the US, Africa, Canada, the Caribbean and Asia. His journalist career which has spanned the last three decades has taken him around the world interviewing artists and world leaders. He is the author of several books covering a wide array of topics. Most recently, he has co-written the very popular series on Hip Hop Culture *Nation Conscious Rap, Twisted Tales on the Hip Hop Streets of Philly, Street Conscious Rap* and the latest release *Tha Global Cipha: Hip Hop Culture and Consciousness* www.globalcipha.com

Andrew Exum is a Soref fellow at The Washington Institute, focusing on contemporary Middle Eastern insurgencies and counterinsurgency strategies. Mr. Exum served in the U.S. Army from 2000 to 2004, leaving active duty as a captain. He was decorated for valor in 2002 while leading a platoon of light infantry in Afghanistan. Subsequently, he led a platoon of Army Rangers into Iraq in 2003 and into Afghanistan in 2004. Mr. Exum has a master's degree in Middle Eastern Studies from the American University of Beirut and continued to study Arabic in 2006 while living in Cairo. The author of the acclaimed book *This Man's Army*, an autobiography of his experience as an officer leading troops in the Afghanistan theater of the war on terror, he has published four op-eds in the *New York Times*, and is currently working on a diplomatic history of U.S.-Iraqi relations in the decade 1991–2001

Rev. Debbie Little-Wyman is the founder of Ecclesia Ministries and Common Cathedral in Boston, which welcome homeless and housed people in Bible Study, art, healing groups, and teaching. She is the author of Home Care for the Dying (1985).

Brooke Beck, BSN RN, graduated in 2001 from the University of Pennsylvania School of Nursing. Brooke spent significant time overseas within the last 4 years in Jordan, Israel, Palestine, Afghanistan, Iraq and most recently the Darfur region of Sudan. She served on various medical teams reaching out to the poverty stricken populations of those countries. Her heart and passion is to bring the highest quality of health care and education to the people of developing nations and, more importantly, to bring the light and truth of Jesus Christ as she lives and works among them. Brooke is also committed to educating people in America about the plight of these nations in order to motivate them to get involved and take action against poverty in the developing world.

Rev. Erik Williams, born and raised in a working-class family in West Philadelphia, Erik J. Williams is a graduate of the University of Pennsylvania, Georgetown University Law Center and Harvard Divinity School. Formerly a minister in both the Baptist and the United Methodist faith traditions, Mr. Williams is currently working outside the parameters of orthodox religious traditions and developing cutting-edge, multi-dimensional models of faith expressions. Previously a criminal defense attorney in Miami, Florida, Mr. Williams is the founder of the Holy House of Thugs, an urban outreach ministry called to address the spiritual needs of those who feel locked out of traditional church settings. Mr. Williams is also the creator of a dynamic, Hip-Hop-centered theology known as *Thugology* or "Thug" Theology. Mr. Williams has written several articles and delivered numerous sermons and lectures on this innovative theology. For more information on the Holy House of Thugs or Thugology, visit www.thugology.com.

Professor Beth Lyon, Esq., received her MS from the Georgetown University School of Foreign Service and her JD from the Georgetown University Law Center. At Georgetown, she was the managing editor of *Law and Policy in International Business*. In 2001, she founded Villanova University Law School's Farmworker Legal Aid Clinic. Before joining the faculty of Villanova University's School of Law, she was a staff attorney with the Lawyers Committee for Human Rights in Washington, D.C., a consultant to the Centre on Housing Rights and Evictions in Geneva, Switzerland, and a Practitioner-in-Residence at the Washington College of Law, American University. She has also published widely on international human rights and the rights of immigrants. She serves on the boards of Latina/Latino Critical Theory, Inc. The Society of American Law Teachers, Friends of Farmworkers, and Global Workers Justice Alliance.

Rev. Charles Lattimore Howard has been serving homeless populations for more than a decade. His various roles in the battle against homelessness include that of an outreach worker (for the City of Philadelphia and for Project H.O.M.E., a nationally recognized non-profit organization in Philadelphia) and that of an educator (preaching, lecturing, and leading workshops on topics related to homelessness). After earning degrees from the University of Pennsylvania and Andover Newton Theological School, Rev. Howard was ordained to the Ministry. He has preached in churches all over the east coast and has given lectures at a number of schools in the area, and is presently working toward his PhD at Lutheran Theological Seminary. He is the Associate Chaplain at the University of Pennsylvania. He has published several articles on topics that include homelessness, faith, and hip-hop culture. His work is featured in the recently released hip-hop volume, *The Global Cipha* by James Spady. He is a founding member of Greater Love Movement.

ABOUT GREATER LOVE MOVEMENT

Greater Love Movement is a pastoral and educational organization seeking to serve as a healing movement of mutual learning for individual and societal transformation around issues related to poverty. They also direct the Greater Love Institute—an experiential internship program for students interested in learning more about and exploring ideas that will help to alleviate poverty.

Greater Love Movement is a non-profit and tax exempt 501 (c) 3 organization. For more information, please visit www.greaterlovemovement.org.

ABOUT PEACE OF MUSIC

Peace of Music is a full-scale music production company specializing in complete project implementation for music professionals and businesses. They also direct the CODA Program. The CODA (Community Outreach, Development, and Achievement) Program is dedicated to providing quality youth music programs and consulting services that empower not only our children but the community as a whole. They aim to bring not only an educational and entertaining experience but a long-lasting and rewarding one. For more information, please visit www.apeaceofmusic.com.